MW01110427

American Billionaires

PRIVILEGE, POLITICS AND POWER

THE NEW YORK TIMES EDITORIAL STAFF

Published in 2021 by New York Times Educational Publishing
in association with The Rosen Publishing Group, Inc.
29 East 21st Street, New York, NY 10010

First Edition

The New York Times
Caroline Que: Editorial Director, Book Development
Phyllis Collazo: Photo Rights/Permissions Editor
Heidi Giovine: Administrative Manager

Rosen Publishing
Megan Kellerman: Managing Editor
Julia Bosson: Editor
Greg Tucker: Creative Director
Brian Garvey: Art Director

Cataloging-in-Publication Data
Names: New York Times Company.
Title: American billionaires: privilege, politics and power / edited
by the New York Times editorial staff.
Description: New York : New York Times Educational Publishing,
2021. | Series: In the headlines | Includes glossary and index.
Identifiers: ISBN 9781642823363 (library bound) | ISBN
9781642823356 (pbk.) | ISBN 9781642823370 (ebook)
Subjects: LCSH: Billionaires—Political activity—United States. |
Rich people—Political activity—United States. | Wealth—Political
aspects. | United States—Politics and government—21st century.
Classification: LCC HC79.W4 A475 2021 |
DDC 320.973086'21—dc23

Manufactured in the United States of America

On the cover: As of 2019, there are more than 600 billionaires
in the United States, ranging from tech moguls to hedge fund
managers and C.E.O.s; Dmitry Rukhlenko/Shutterstock.

Contents

CHAPTER 3

Liberal Powerhouses:
Warren Buffett and George Soros

CHAPTER 4

Conservative Billionaires:
The Kochs, the Mercers and the DeVos Family

Introduction

IN 2019, the Democratic Presidential primary candidate Bernie Sanders sent out a tweet that grabbed headlines. "Billionaires should not exist," he wrote, articulating the principle that undergirded his proposal for a wealth tax, which would take aim at the ultra-rich by targeting the full extent of their fortunes.

Sanders was articulating an idea that has gained increased traction in recent years, particularly among the Democratic base. Inspired in part by Sanders's own outspoken refrain on economic inequality, it has become a common refrain that the top 1 percent of earners control a vastly disproportionate amount of wealth in the American economy. Some C.E.O.s earn thousands of times more than their average employees in wages alone, resulting in an economy where the wealthiest exponentially outpace low- and middle-earners. And as policies put forth by the Trump administration further slash the tax rates of the ultra-rich, it seems likely these dynasties of wealth will continue for generations to come.

The line between billionaires and celebrities has blurred in American culture. To many, they represent the apex of the American dream, the product of hard work, innovation and creative vision. Each generation has produced its own set of billionaires: investors like Warren Buffett; hedge fund managers like George Soros; the family of Walmart founder Sam Walton; tech entrepreneurs like Bill Gates and Mark Zuckerberg. The contributions of these individuals have bolstered the economy, and their innovations have reshaped American culture, technology and real estate.

At the same time, the existence of these billionaires and their wealth has begun to attract increased scrutiny by activists and reformers

MICHAEL APPLETON FOR THE NEW YORK TIMES

Jeff Bezos, founder and chief executive of Amazon, during a news conference unveiling the Kindle 2 in 2009.

alike. The economic growth that the United States experienced in the latter half of the twentieth century and the beginning of the twenty-first largely accelerated economic inequality rather than resolving it. While Jeff Bezos's Amazon, based in Seattle, became the second company to reach a valuation of one trillion dollars, allowing him to surpass Bill Gates as America's richest man, Seattle's homeless population surged in the last decade. In American history, there has arguably never been such a stark division between the nation's wealthiest and the nation's poorest.

Reformers argue that billionaires can only build their businesses with the use of nationally subsidized highways and public transportation, and point to the ways that a "wealth tax" could support much needed public works projects. Critics have also argued that inherited wealth and demographic biases have made the dream of reaching the billionaire class remote for those not already inside of it. Statistically speaking, American billionaires are overwhelmingly white and male; there are few women of color, and Oprah Winfrey is the only black woman on Forbes's list of America's wealthiest people.

But billionaires point to their long history of philanthropy. Most have created philanthropic foundations that pour money into a variety of worthy causes, led by the model of Warren Buffett, who has pledged the majority of his fortune to charity. The Bill & Melinda Gates Foundation is now the largest private foundation in the world, while the Chan Zuckerberg Initiative has begun to invest in areas of health and education development.

Billionaires also put their money into political causes with massive implications. Families like the Koch brothers, the Mercers and the DeVoses have poured millions of dollars into supporting conservative policies. Others, like George Soros, have made massive contributions to liberal causes. The influence that this affords the billionaire class has opened up a debate on both sides of the aisle as to the extent to which individuals should be able to impact the workings of American democracy.

The moral, social and economic implications of the billionaire class will be debated in America for decades to come. In the meantime, as the articles in this book demonstrate, there is more work to be done to scrutinize both the means and the extent of accumulated wealth, as well as how it translates into power in determining the nation's social, economic and political landscape.

CHAPTER 1

The World of the Superrich

It can be hard to conceive of the level of wealth actually held by the ultra-rich. To put it in perspective, Jeff Bezos's net worth, around $120,000,000,000, is more than the individual G.D.P.s of nearly 100 countries. The articles in this chapter introduce the economic and political circumstances that paved the way for the billionaire class, examining the spread of its influence and extent of its power. They also pose one of the key questions of our time: Should anyone have the right to be a billionaire?

A Quiet Meeting of America's Very Richest

BY A. G. SULZBERGER | MAY 20, 2009

THERE ARE FEWER billionaires in these tough economic times, so one might imagine that the remaining ones would attract more attention when they moved en masse. Yet when some of America's most prominent capitalists met earlier this month at Rockefeller University, it took weeks before anyone noticed.

The secrecy continued even after IrishCentral.com, a Web site focused on Irish-American news, wrote on Monday about the May 5 gathering, reporting that the group discussed charitable giving.

Participants steadfastly refused to reveal details about the meeting, citing an agreement to protect the confidentiality of the discussion.

Mayor Michael R. Bloomberg, who was there, revealed little in a brusque response to a question on Wednesday afternoon. "Anytime I have a meeting that's not on the public schedule, it's not going to be on the public schedule," he said.

Spokesmen for the other participants declined to comment.

The silence fed the conspiracy theories that so often emerge when powerful people meet behind closed doors, particularly when the invitation list seems pulled from the Forbes rankings of the world's wealthiest people.

The group included Bill Gates (1); Warren E. Buffett (2); Mayor Bloomberg (17); George Soros (29); the real estate developer Eli Broad (93) and his wife, Edythe; Oprah Winfrey (234); David Rockefeller Sr. (305) and his son David Rockefeller Jr.; Ted Turner (376); Peter G. Peterson (430), co-founder of the Blackstone Group, the private equity firm; Julian H. Robertson Jr. (559), who ran a prominent hedge fund; and John P. Morgridge (647), former chairman of Cisco Systems, and his wife, Tashia.

Based on February estimates by Forbes, the room had a net worth of about $120 billion, or nearly as much as New York State's annual budget.

The participants have reputations as outsize philanthropists, and many have teamed up on causes. Mr. Buffett, for example, recently pledged to donate the bulk of his fortune, currently estimated at $37 billion, to the Bill and Melinda Gates Foundation. Together, the men and women at the meeting had donated more than $72.5 billion to charitable causes since 1996, according to an estimate by The Chronicle of Philanthropy.

On Wednesday afternoon, the silence was finally broken when one of the participants, Patricia Q. Stonesifer, former chief executive of the Gates Foundation and current chairwoman of the Smithsonian Institution, said the others had been concerned about privacy, not secrecy.

"Various members of the group have been talking about philanthropy," she said. "This is a time when the needs are great. So it seemed like a really good time to get together."

The event was jointly conceived by Mr. Buffett, Mr. Gates and the elder Mr. Rockefeller, Ms. Stonesifer said. "This was the first time this particular group had come together and shared a table," she said, but added that with their charitable activities and general prominence, "the degrees of separation were few."

The gathering started at 3 p.m. on May 5 and lasted through dinner, and was held at the Rockefeller University president's residence on the Upper East Side campus, said Joseph Bonner, a university spokesman. The president, Paul Nurse, was out of town; the university became involved when the elder Mr. Rockefeller, its former chairman, asked that it provide space for the meeting, Mr. Bonner said.

The discussions centered on charitable giving, and participants talked about their personal causes, told of lessons they had learned, and suggested ways to improve and increase philanthropic efforts, Ms. Stonesifer said.

"There wasn't a set agenda. It was a discussion," Ms. Stonesifer said. "The areas of discussion were as varied as the individuals there and their interests."

No specific plans came out of the meeting, nor were plans made to meet again, Ms. Stonesifer said, adding, "They really all wanted to continue that dialogue."

Billionaires to the Barricades

OPINION | BY ALAN FEUER | JULY 3, 2015

EARLIER THIS MONTH, when the billionaire merchandising mogul Johann Rupert gave a speech at The Financial Times's "luxury summit" in Monaco, he sounded more like a Marxist theoretician than someone who made his fortune selling Cartier diamonds and Montblanc pens. Appearing before a crowd of executives from Fendi and Ferrari, Mr. Rupert argued that it wasn't right — or even good business — for "the 0.1 percent of the 0.1 percent" to raid the world's spoils. "It's unfair and it is not sustainable," he said.

For several years now, populist politicians and liberal intellectuals have been inveighing against income inequality, an issue that is gaining traction among the broader body politic, as shown by a recent New York Times/CBS News poll that found that nearly 60 percent of American voters want their government to do more to reduce the gap between the rich and the poor. But in the last several months, this topic has been taken up by a different and unlikely group of advocates: a small but vocal band of billionaires.

In March, for instance, Paul Tudor Jones II, the private equity investor, gave a TED talk in which he proclaimed that the divide between the top 1 percent in the United States and the remainder of the country "cannot and will not persist." Mr. Jones, who is thought to be worth nearly $5 billion, added that such divides have historically been resolved in one of three ways: taxes, wars or revolution.

A few months earlier, Jeff Greene, a billionaire real estate entrepreneur, suggested on CNBC that the superrich should pay higher taxes in order to restore what he called "the inclusive economy that I grew up in."

And in June, Nick Hanauer, a tech billionaire from Seattle, wrote a blog post laying out the capitalist's case for a $15 minimum wage. The post echoed sentiments that Mr. Hanauer made in a separate polemic he wrote last summer for Politico, in which he addressed himself directly to the planet's "zillionaires" and said: "I have a message for my fellow filthy rich, for all of us who live in our gated bubble worlds: Wake up, people. It won't last."

What's going on here? Are all these anxious magnates really interested in leveling the playing field or are they simply paying lip service to a shift in the political winds? Or perhaps it's just a statistical blip, given that most of the world's 1,800 billionaires are not exactly out at the barricades lifting pitchforks for economic change.

According to Chrystia Freeland, author of the 2012 book "Plutocrats: The Rise of the New Global Super Rich and the Fall of Everyone Else," the phenomenon of the socially conscious billionaire is significant and good. "It is absolutely happening," Ms. Freeland said. "After my book came out, a few billionaires quietly got in touch with me to say that they agreed that the current system isn't working. It makes sense that the people who have benefited most from the economy have the greatest interest in making it sustainable."

Ms. Freeland, who is also a Liberal Party member of the Canadian Parliament, pointed to the so-called Conference on Inclusive Capitalism, organized in London last year by Lynn Forester de Rothschild, a member of the storied Rothschild banking clan. While the one-day event was derided by some as a nervous hedge against the threat of insurrection, the ostensible purpose of the gathering was to reorient the 1 percent toward public-minded goods like long-term investing, environmental stewardship and the fate of the global working class.

Financiers like George Soros and Warren E. Buffett have trod this ground before to great attention, but now that other billionaires have been moved to join them, it has helped to change the conversation, said Darrell M. West, a scholar at the Brookings Institution and the author of "Billionaires: Reflections on the Upper Crust."

"The messenger matters," Mr. West said. "When people of modest means complain about inequality, it usually gets written off as class warfare, but when billionaires complain, the problem is redefined" — in a helpful way, he added — "as basic fairness and economic sustainability."

This is not to say that the current crop of concerned tycoons is working purely out of altruistic motives. "There's been a major backlash against inequality," Mr. West said. "And some wealthy individuals have felt a pressure to address it."

Given the political groundswell for decreasing wealth disparity, Mr. West added, "There's a realization among the billionaire class that it's actually in their own self-interest to at least spread some of the wealth around."

Of course, it may be that some of these outspoken billionaires are not responding to politics so much as playing it themselves. "I'm not surprised to hear the wealthy saying these things, but talk is cheap," said Dennis Kelleher, the president of Better Markets, which advocates financial reform. "These people know exactly how to move the levers of power and, until that happens, whatever they say is nothing but empty words."

According to William D. Cohan, a former Wall Street banker who has written frequently about billionaires, if the investor class were truly interested in targeting unfairness, its members would try to alter the policies of the Federal Reserve, which tend to help the rich, or do away with inequity-inducing programs like tax incentives for hedge funds.

Mr. Cohan said that proposals like increasing the minimum wage, a popular rallying cry among those decrying income inequality, would have, at best, a minimal effect on reducing the rift between ordinary people and the 1 percent.

Most billionaires, he added, are apt to address inequality by donating portions of their fortunes, not by seeking systemic economic change. "Charity? Yes," Mr. Cohan said. "But leveling the playing field? No."

And yet the extremely wealthy do face an abiding risk from festering inequity: The have-nots might finally lose patience and turn upon the haves.

"That's the real danger," Mr. Cohan said. "This little thing called the French Revolution."

ALAN FEUER is a metropolitan reporter for The New York Times.

Privilege, Pathology and Power

OPINION | BY PAUL KRUGMAN | JAN. 1, 2016

WEALTH CAN BE BAD for your soul. That's not just a hoary piece of folk wisdom; it's a conclusion from serious social science, confirmed by statistical analysis and experiment. The affluent are, on average, less likely to exhibit empathy, less likely to respect norms and even laws, more likely to cheat, than those occupying lower rungs on the economic ladder.

And it's obvious, even if we don't have statistical confirmation, that extreme wealth can do extreme spiritual damage. Take someone whose personality might have been merely disagreeable under normal circumstances, and give him the kind of wealth that lets him surround himself with sycophants and usually get whatever he wants. It's not hard to see how he could become almost pathologically self-regarding and unconcerned with others. So what happens to a nation that gives ever-growing political power to the superrich?

Modern America is a society in which a growing share of income and wealth is concentrated in the hands of a small number of people, and these people have huge political influence — in the early stages of the 2016 presidential campaign, around half the contributions came from fewer than 200 wealthy families. The usual concern about this march toward oligarchy is that the interests and policy preferences of the very rich are quite different from those of the population at large, and that is surely the biggest problem.

But it's also true that those empowered by money-driven politics include a disproportionate number of spoiled egomaniacs. Which brings me to the current election cycle.

The most obvious illustration of the point I've been making is the man now leading the Republican field. Donald Trump would probably have been a blowhard and a bully whatever his social station. But his billions have insulated him from the external checks that limit most people's ability to act out their narcissistic tendencies; nobody has ever been in a position to tell him, "You're fired!" And the result is the face you keep seeing on your TV.

But Mr. Trump isn't the only awesomely self-centered billionaire playing an outsized role in the 2016 campaign.

There have been some interesting news reports lately about Sheldon Adelson, the Las Vegas gambling magnate. Mr. Adelson has been involved in some fairly complex court proceedings, which revolve around claims of misconduct in his operations in Macau, including links to organized crime and prostitution. Given his business, this may not be all that surprising. What was surprising was his behavior in court, where he refused to answer routine questions and argued with the judge, Elizabeth Gonzales. That, as she rightly pointed out, isn't something witnesses get to do.

Then Mr. Adelson bought Nevada's largest newspaper. As the sale was being finalized, reporters at the paper were told to drop everything and start monitoring all activity of three judges, including Ms. Gonzales. And while the paper never published any results from that investigation, an attack on Judge Gonzales, with what looks like a fictitious byline, did appear in a small Connecticut newspaper owned by one of Mr. Adelson's associates.

O.K., but why do we care? Because Mr. Adelson's political spending has made him a huge player in Republican politics — so much so that reporters routinely talk about the "Adelson primary," in which candidates trek to Las Vegas to pay obeisance.

Are there other cases? Yes indeed, even if the egomania doesn't rise to Adelson levels. I find myself thinking, for example, of the hedge-fund billionaire Paul Singer, another big power in the G.O.P., who published an investor's letter declaring that inflation was running rampant — he could tell from the prices of Hamptons real estate and high-end art. Economists got some laughs out of the incident, but think of the self-absorption required to write something like that without realizing how it would sound to non-billionaires.

Or think of the various billionaires who, a few years ago, were declaring with straight faces, and no sign of self-awareness, that President Obama was holding back the economy by suggesting that some businesspeople had misbehaved. You see, he was hurting their feelings.

Just to be clear, the biggest reason to oppose the power of money in politics is the way it lets the wealthy rig the system and distort policy priorities. And the biggest reason billionaires hate Mr. Obama is what he did to their taxes, not their feelings. The fact that some of those buying influence are also horrible people is secondary.

But it's not trivial. Oligarchy, rule by the few, also tends to become rule by the monstrously self-centered. Narcisstocracy? Jerkigarchy? Anyway, it's an ugly spectacle, and it's probably going to get even uglier over the course of the year ahead.

PAUL KRUGMAN joined The New York Times in 1999 as an Op-Ed columnist. In 2008, Mr. Krugman was the sole recipient of the Nobel Memorial Prize in Economic Sciences for his work on international trade theory.

World's 8 Richest Have as Much Wealth as Bottom Half, Oxfam Says

BY GERRY MULLANY | JAN. 16, 2017

HOW CONCENTRATED HAS wealth become in the globalized modern world? Here's one answer: Just eight of the richest people on earth own as much combined wealth as half the human race.

That's a notable change from last year, when it was reckoned to take 62 of the superrich to match the assets of the 3.6 billion people in the poorer half of mankind.

The charity Oxfam does the math each year and publishes its results just in time for the World Economic Forum in Davos, Switzerland, where many of the spectacularly wealthy are often among the attendees, along with diplomats, political figures, and business and cultural leaders. The Oxfam report on inequality is on the agenda for discussion at the forum.

Oxfam bases its figures in part on Forbes's annual list of billionaires and the magazine's estimates of their wealth. This year, Oxfam said, new data gathered by Credit Suisse about the global poor led it to lower its estimates of their assets, and revise its findings about how few rich men — the eight are all men — were needed to equal the wealth of 3.6 billion people.

Here are the eight, with their net worth as estimated by Forbes, whose annual survey depends on a range of sources:

Bill Gates, the founder of Microsoft, led the list with a net worth of $75 billion. He is scheduled to speak at the forum in Davos this year.

Amancio Ortega Gaona, the Spanish founder of the fashion company Inditex, best known for its oldest and biggest brand, Zara, has a net worth of $67 billion.

Warren E. Buffett, the chairman of Berkshire Hathaway, $60.8 billion.

Carlos Slim Helú, the Mexican telecommunications magnate, $50 billion.

Jeff Bezos, the founder of Amazon, $45.2 billion.

Mark Zuckerberg, Facebook's creator, $44.6 billion.

Lawrence J. Ellison, the founder of Oracle, $43.6 billion.

Michael R. Bloomberg, the former mayor of New York and founder of the media and financial-data giant Bloomberg L.L.P., $40 billion.

Where the Billionaires Come From

BY MICHAEL CORKERY | FEB. 19, 2017

IN THE EARLY 20th century, a young journalist named Napoleon Hill embarked on the assignment of a lifetime.

Mr. Hill set out to study hundreds of the nation's most successful people and write a book about how they became so accomplished.

Mr. Hill spent two decades analyzing the life stories, strategies and personal philosophies of entrepreneurs and industrialists like Henry Ford, William Wrigley and John D. Rockefeller.

The resulting book, "Think and Grow Rich," was published in 1937 and became a self-help guide for everyday Americans seeking great wealth.

Mr. Hill tried to convince his readers — many of them emotionally and financially battered by the Great Depression — that with the right attitude they, too, could amass a fortune.

"One must realize that all who have accumulated great fortunes first did a certain amount of dreaming, hoping, wishing, desiring and planning before they acquired money," Mr. Hill wrote.

Eighty years later, Mr. Hill's egalitarian notions seem to ring hollow on many levels. There is a troublingly wide gap between the economic fortunes of the rich and the poor — an inequality that has helped unleash political populism in Europe and the United States. (Ironically, President Trump, a self-proclaimed billionaire, rode that resentment to the White House.)

The idea that the secret to great wealth comes from a combination of discipline, perseverance and belief in yourself sounds Pollyanna-ish in an era of widespread disillusionment with how the economy and society actually works.

Indeed, the chance of becoming a billionaire remains incredibly slim. Wealth-X, a research firm that tracks global wealth, said there were 2,473 billionaires in 2015, an increase of 148 from the year before and about 0.00003 percent of the world's 7.3 billion people.

In "Think and Grow Rich," Napoleon Hill sought to explain how entrepreneurs like Henry Ford — shown in a photograph from around 1898 — found success.

Still, an optimist like Mr. Hill, who died in 1970, might take heart in one data point from Wealth-X: More than half of the world's billionaires are self-made.

And that number is increasing. Self-made billionaires represent 57 percent of total billionaire wealth, or more than $4.3 trillion, a figure that was up 7 percent from 2014. Meanwhile, the number of billionaires with inherited wealth — 323, according to Wealth-X — fell by 29 percent from 2014.

The booming technology sector has minted many of the recent self-made titans — entrepreneurs like Travis Kalanick, a co-founder and the chief executive of Uber, and the co-founders of Airbnb, Brian Chesky, Joe Gebbia and Nathan Blecharczyk.

"Many people have great ideas. But to grow an idea into a huge business is a different matter," said Maya Imberg, custom research director at Wealth-X. "Billionaires tend to be incredibly focused."

In his book, Mr. Hill tried to show that qualities like focus and perseverance were within everyone.

He told the story of how Thomas Edison failed thousands of times before he perfected the incandescent electric light bulb and how Henry Ford pushed his engineers to develop the V-8 motor despite the technical challenges.

"A thousand people could be pointed out who have a better education than Ford's, yet they live in poverty because they do not possess the right plan for the accumulation of money," Mr. Hill wrote.

Wealth-X is the big data equivalent to Mr. Hill's one-man reporting project. The firm employs about 150 researchers across the world who collect and analyze data about the richest people.

Based on that data, you may have a slightly better chance of becoming a billionaire if you went to Harvard, which was the most popular school among billionaires by a wide margin. (Stanford came in second.)

Engineering degrees were the most popular among billionaires, followed by business, according to Approved Index, another firm that researches the wealthy. There are some notable billionaires with humanities degrees, like the financier Carl Icahn, who majored in philosophy at Princeton. Jack Ma, founder of the Chinese e-commerce giant Alibaba, has a teaching degree.

It is well known that Mark Zuckerberg of Facebook and Bill Gates of Microsoft dropped out of Harvard to start their businesses. But they are not alone. About 30 percent of the world's billionaires never obtain a college degree.

"It is counterintuitive to what you are told growing up," said Grace Garland, head of research at Approved Index.

If the sheer numbers are any guide, your chances of becoming a billionaire as a woman are especially remote. In 2015, 140 of the 148 people who broke into the billionaire ranks were men. All of the top 10 billionaires are men, according to Wealth-X.

And yet for all the male-dominated, Ivy League exclusivity of the billionaire's club, self-help gurus and ordinary people continue to pore over the biographies and public statements of the ultrawealthy, looking for the secret sauce.

Andrew Collins, 37, the founder of a sports marketing company in China, has noted the reading habits of billionaires.

Elon Musk, the chief executive of Tesla and SpaceX, and the investor Warren E. Buffett are said to be avid readers. Mr. Gates once said that "reading is still the main way that I both learn new things and test my understanding."

In a recent interview with Forbes, Mr. Gates' father, William H. Gates Sr., said his son devoured all kinds of books as a boy, including encyclopedias and science fiction. "I was thrilled that my child was such an avid reader, but he read so much that Bill's mother and I had to institute a rule: no books at the dinner table," he said.

Mr. Collins said many of these wealthy men had parents who helped them to succeed.

Mr. Gates' parents arranged for him to take time off from classes during his senior year in high school to work on code for the electrical grid management system at a local power plant.

Richard Branson, the billionaire founder of Virgin Group, said his father, a lawyer, taught him the importance of dreaming big and instilled in him a desire for excellence.

In a tribute to him, Mr. Branson wrote: "another lesson I learned from my father, which has greatly impacted my career, was: 'If a job's worth doing, it's worth doing well.' This, one of his favorite sayings, was ingrained in me from an early age."

Mr. Collins said that while he was growing up in Australia, his father made him read "Think and Grow Rich," and taught him how to think about making money in different ways to accumulate wealth.

"The people who say that entrepreneurs are born, that is ridiculous. They are made," he said.

"You need grit and unwavering personal confidence. Those are nonnegotiable in a billionaire," he said.

Giving Away Billions as Fast as They Can

BY DAVID GELLES | OCT. 20, 2017

STEP ASIDE, ROCKEFELLER. Move over, Carnegie. Out of the way, Ford.

For the better part of a century, a few Gilded Age names dominated the ranks of big philanthropy.

No longer.

In a matter of years, a new crop of ultra-wealthy Americans has eclipsed the old guard of philanthropic titans. With names like Soros, Gates, Bloomberg, Mercer, Koch and Zuckerberg, these new megadonors are upending long-established norms in the staid world of big philanthropy.

They have accumulated vast fortunes early in their lives. They are spending it faster and writing bigger checks. And they are increasingly willing to take on hot-button social and political issues — on the right and left — that thrust them into the center of contentious debates.

Plenty of billionaires are still buying sports teams, building yachts and donating to museums and hospitals. But many new philanthropists appear less interested in naming a business school after themselves than in changing the world.

"They have a problem-solving mentality rather than a stewardship mentality," said David Callahan, founder of the website Inside Philanthropy and author of "The Givers," a book about today's major donors. "They are not saving their money for a rainy day. They want to have impact now."

George Soros, the hedge fund billionaire and Democratic donor, recently made public the transfer of some $18 billion to his Open Society Foundations, a sprawling effort to promote democracy and combat intolerance around the world. The gift, which essentially endowed Open Society in perpetuity, made it the second largest foundation by assets in the country. The only philanthropy with more resources is the Bill and Melinda Gates Foundation.

"We're seeing a real changing of the guard," said Mr. Callahan. "The top foundations, especially measured by annual giving, are more and more piloted by people who are alive."

Having made billions and shaped the world with their companies, this new guard is setting lofty goals as they prepare to give their fortunes away. Take the Chan Zuckerberg Initiative, established by the Facebook co-founder Mark Zuckerberg and his wife Priscilla Chan. It is not looking to merely improve health in the developing world. One of its aspirations is to help "cure, prevent, or manage all diseases by the end of the century."

That may sound like good news all around. If a handful of billionaires want to spend their fortunes saving lives, why not simply applaud them? But as their ambitions grow, so too does their influence, meaning that for better or worse, a few billionaires are wielding considerable influence over everything from medical research to social policy to politics.

"This isn't the government collecting taxes and deciding which social problems it wants to solve through a democratic process," said Eileen Heisman, chief executive of the National Philanthropic Trust, a nonprofit that works with foundations. "This is a small group of people, who have made way more money than they need, deciding what issues they care about. That affects us all."

IDEAS AND IDEALS

In 2015, at the ripe old age of 31, Mr. Zuckerberg made a momentous decision. He and Ms. Chan had just welcomed their first daughter into the world. Soon after, they pledged to give away 99 percent of their Facebook shares, then valued at some $45 billion, in their lifetime. "Our society has an obligation to invest now to improve the lives of all those coming into this world, not just those already here," they wrote in a letter addressed to their daughter, posted on Facebook.

Nearly two years later, the Chan Zuckerberg Initiative is taking shape. Structured as a limited liability corporation rather than a traditional foundation, a move the founders say gives them more flexibility, the organization is focused on three main areas: science, education and justice.

Already, the couple has committed more than half a billion dollars to create a nonprofit research center giving unrestricted funding to physicians, scientists and engineers from top California universities. They support an effort to map and identify all the cells in a healthy human body. And late last year, they pledged to spend $3 billion on preventing, curing and managing "all disease by the end of the century."

In considering how to deploy his billions, Mr. Zuckerberg was no doubt inspired by his friend and mentor, the Microsoft co-founder Mr. Gates. Since its founding in 2000, the Gates Foundation has established itself as a force without peer in big philanthropy. Not only does it have the largest endowment of any foundation, some $40 billion, but it also spends more each year, nearly $5.5 billion in 2016 alone.

The Gates's efforts are sprawling, spanning the globe and crossing fields. Their foundation funds efforts to reduce tobacco use, combat H.I.V. and improve education in Washington state. It has spent billions to reduce the spread of infectious diseases and malaria. And its efforts have already helped a coalition of world health organizations all but eradicate polio.

Mr. Soros's foundation differs in important ways. Rather than try to solve discrete problems like disease, Open Society aims to promote values like democracy, tolerance and inclusion, which Mr. Soros, a Holocaust survivor, holds dear. In practice, this means that his money is less likely to fund early stage medical research, and more likely to help refugees displaced by conflict.

But while the issues they address are distinct, the broad outline of these billionaires' efforts have much in common: shaping the world in their moral image. "It is not called the Soros Foundation," said Patrick Gaspard, the incoming president of the Open Society Foundations.

"George approaches this philanthropic effort without an eye toward the preservation of his reputation and legacy, but with a fierce determination around the protection of these ideas and ideals."

Big foundations have been making an impact since long before Mr. Gates came around, of course. In 1943, for example, the Rockefeller Foundation began working with the Mexican government in hopes of improving the country's agricultural industry. That work spurred the "Green Revolution," which has boosted crop yields across the developing world. The Ford Foundation helped establish the microfinance industry, partnering with Muhammad Yunus to launch the Grameen Bank.

And in recent years, some older foundations have refocused their efforts on tackling big issues.

Today, the Ford Foundation is focused on reducing inequality, and the John D. and Catherine T. MacArthur Foundation is focusing on "big bets" including combating climate change. But those legacy foundations are now largely guided by stewards, not the billionaires with their names on the door. Mr. Gates, Mr. Zuckerberg, Mr. Bloomberg and Mr. Soros are personally engaged in their foundations, and willing to court controversy.

POLARIZED POLITICS

When news of Mr. Soros's $18 billion transfer of wealth to the Open Society Foundations was announced, reaction from conservatives was swift and predictable. Fox News called him an "Uber-liberal billionaire." Breitbart News said the gift "makes his organization the biggest player on the American political scene," adding that "the foundation's work has supported dogmatic, aggressive left-wing groups that disrupt liberal democracy and stifle opposing voices."

Mr. Soros became a lightning rod for conservative criticism largely because of his own political contributions rather than his foundation's spending. He was a major donor to Hillary Clinton, and spent millions of dollars on efforts to defeat Donald J. Trump in last year's presidential election.

Yet he is equally reviled in certain circles for his philanthropic work. Since the 1990s, Mr. Soros has used the Open Society Foundations to advance causes that are deeply unpopular with many Republicans, including loosening drug laws, promoting gay rights and calling attention to abuses by the police.

Mr. Gaspard of the Open Society Foundations asserts that Mr. Soros is not courting controversy. Rather, he said, Mr. Soros is simply on the right side of history. "The rights of the Jewish community in 1937 in Berlin may have been deemed controversial by some in that society, but we all appreciate today the inherent value in that fight," he said. "The same is true today, when we are involved in safe needle transfers for drug addicts, or when we're engaged in supporting the rights of sex workers in Johannesburg, or the Rohingya in Myanmar."

Michael Bloomberg, the former New York mayor, is also no stranger to criticism. The purpose of his foundation, Bloomberg Philanthropies, is to "ensure better, longer lives for the greatest number of people." In practice, this has meant Mr. Bloomberg spending hundreds of millions of dollars on issues including gun control and obesity prevention, drawing the ire of Republicans who oppose what they see as excessive regulation.

Even the Gates Foundation, which is "dedicated to improving the quality of life for individuals around the world," sometimes finds itself drawn into the culture wars. Global Justice Now, an advocacy organization based in London, said in a report that the Gates Foundation is "not a neutral, charitable strategy for which the world should be thankful" but "a specific ideological strategy that promotes neo-liberal economic policies."

This isn't the first time philanthropy has been politicized. A century ago, Julius Rosenwald, a part owner of Sears Roebuck & Company, emerged as a champion of African Americans. Mr. Rosenwald, a Jewish businessman from Chicago, befriended the black educator Booker T. Washington and began funding the construction of schools for African Americans across the Jim Crow South. When the Ku Klux

Klan burned down his schools, he simply rebuilt them. In doing so, Mr. Rosenwald made enemies.

"Julius Rosenwald was the first social justice philanthropist," said Darren Walker, president of the Ford Foundation. "He upset all of the powers in the South."

That, in Mr. Walker's estimation, was a good thing. And today, Mr. Walker is encouraging donors to find their inner Julius Rosenwald. "Philanthropy should not be an expression of only one's wealth and power," he said. "It also needs to be an expression of humility and an expression of skepticism about some of the very systems and structures that produced one's wealth. What I hope for is that more philanthropists in this generation understand the difference between generosity and justice."

There are equally powerful forces flexing their financial muscles on both sides of the political spectrum. And, like Mr. Soros, conservatives are using both foundations and political donations to achieve their goals.

Though the brothers Charles and David Koch are best known for their work supporting Republicans, they also fund a network of philanthropies that support efforts to, among other things, question climate change and encourage conservative thinking on college campuses. The Mercer Family Foundation, run by Rebekah Mercer, a prominent supporter of President Trump, has bankrolled conservative think tanks including the Heritage Foundation and the Heartland Institute.

"The wealthy have become more polarized along with the rest of America," said Mr. Callahan. "You have more liberal, progressive wealthy people than ever before. Meanwhile, you have lots of conservative rich people. There's this escalating arms race among mega donors."

IMPATIENT OPTIMISTS

John D. MacArthur made a fortune in the insurance business. But when he set up his foundation near the end of his life in the 1970s, he didn't have strong views on what purpose it should serve. "I figured out how to make the money," he reportedly said to one of his foundation's original trustees. "You fellows will have to figure out how to spend it."

For the most part, previous generations of billionaires only got serious about giving away their fortunes late in life and that has been changing. "What we're seeing these days is people make so much money with an I.P.O. that being a philanthropist becomes an essential part of your identity in your late 20s," said Benjamin Soskis, who studies the history of philanthropy at the Urban Institute, a think tank in Washington.

So little time, and so much money to dispose of — that is the dilemma for today's mega philanthropists. Mr. Zuckerberg and Ms. Chan say they are committed to giving away their fortune in their lifetime, which is why they are beginning at such a young age. "Giving, like anything else, takes practice to do effectively," Mr. Zuckerberg wrote on Facebook. "So if we want to be good at it in 10-15 years, we should start now."

By starting sooner, Mr. Zuckerberg said his money should go further. "Any good we do will hopefully compound over time," he wrote. "If we can help children get a better education now then they can grow up and help others too in the time we might have otherwise waited to get started."

Mr. Gates and the billionaire investor Warren Buffett launched the Giving Pledge, which asks wealthy people to commit to donating at least half of their fortunes to philanthropic causes during their lifetimes or upon their death. They want their fellow billionaires to act with urgency. On their own website, the Gates' describes themselves as "impatient optimists."

In June, Jeff Bezos, the founder of Amazon.com who, with a net worth of $84 billion or so, briefly supplanted Bill Gates as the richest person in the world this year, asked the public for some advice. "I'm thinking I want much of my philanthropic activity to be helping people in the here and now — short term — at the intersection of urgent need and lasting impact," Mr. Bezos wrote on Twitter. "If you have ideas, just reply to this tweet."

More than 48,000 replies flooded in. Mr. Bezos has not announced what he will do with his many billions, but his request for proposals was a reminder that there are untold fortunes that remain uncommitted to philanthropic causes. Nearly 200 people with a combined worth approaching $1 trillion have signed the Giving Pledge. New billionaires are beginning to ramp up their giving. Laurene Powell Jobs, the widow of Apple co-founder Steve Jobs, recently founded the Emerson Collective, which is putting money toward issues including education and immigration.

And as more people commit their fortunes to philanthropy, there will be many more organizations like the Open Society Foundations, and they may be with us for a long time. "The sun never sets on George Soros's philanthropic empire, and the money is never going to run out," said Mr. Callahan. "His money could still be affecting public policy 300 years from now."

It is the dawn of a new era of big philanthropy. As wealth is rapidly created and concentrated, new mega foundations are being born, each reflecting its founder's priorities. And much as Mr. Soros, Mr. Gates, Mr. Zuckerberg and the others in their cohort have eclipsed the titans of the Gilded Age, they are likely to one day be overtaken by an even newer crop of immensely wealthy and impatient optimists.

Abolish Billionaires

OPINION | BY FARHAD MANJOO | FEB. 6, 2019

A radical idea is gaining adherents on the left. It's the perfect way to blunt tech-driven inequality.

LAST FALL, Tom Scocca, editor of the essential blog Hmm Daily, wrote a tiny, searing post that has been rattling around my head ever since.

"Some ideas about how to make the world better require careful, nuanced thinking about how best to balance competing interests," he began. "Others don't: Billionaires are bad. We should presumptively get rid of billionaires. All of them."

Mr. Scocca — a longtime writer at Gawker until that site was muffled by a billionaire — offered a straightforward argument for knee-capping the wealthiest among us. A billion dollars is wildly more than anyone needs, even accounting for life's most excessive lavishes. It's far more than anyone might reasonably claim to deserve, however much he believes he has contributed to society.

At some level of extreme wealth, money inevitably corrupts. On the left and the right, it buys political power, it silences dissent, it serves primarily to perpetuate ever-greater wealth, often unrelated to any reciprocal social good. For Mr. Scocca, that level is self-evidently somewhere around one billion dollars; beyond that, you're irredeemable.

I cover technology, an industry that belches up a murder of new billionaires annually, and much of my career has required a deep anthropological inquiry into billionairedom. But I'm embarrassed to say I had never before considered Mr. Scocca's idea — that if we aimed, through public and social policy, simply to discourage people from attaining and possessing more than a billion in lucre, just about everyone would be better off.

In my defense, back in October, abolishing billionaires felt way out there. It sounded radical, impossible, maybe even un-American, and even Mr. Scocca seemed to float the notion as a mere reverie.

But it is an illustration of the political precariousness of billionaires that the idea has since become something like mainline thought on the progressive left. Bernie Sanders and Elizabeth Warren are floating new taxes aimed at the superrich, including special rates for billionaires. Representative Alexandria Ocasio-Cortez, who also favors higher taxes on the wealthy, has been making a moral case against the existence of billionaires. Dan Riffle, her policy adviser, recently changed his Twitter name to "Every Billionaire Is A Policy Failure." Last week, HuffPost asked, "Should Billionaires Even Exist?"

I suspect the question is getting so much attention because the answer is obvious: Nope. Billionaires should not exist — at least not in their present numbers, with their current globe-swallowing power, garnering this level of adulation, while the rest of the economy scrapes by.

I like to use this column to explore maximalist policy visions — positions we might aspire to over time rather than push through tomorrow. Abolishing billionaires might not sound like a practical idea, but if you think about it as a long-term goal in light of today's deepest economic ills, it feels anything but radical. Instead, banishing billionaires — seeking to cut their economic power, working to reduce their political power and attempting to question their social status — is a pithy, perfectly encapsulated vision for surviving the digital future.

Billionaire abolishment could take many forms. It could mean preventing people from keeping more than a billion in booty, but more likely it would mean higher marginal taxes on income, wealth and estates for billionaires and people on the way to becoming billionaires. These policy ideas turn out to poll very well, even if they're probably not actually redistributive enough to turn most billionaires into sub-billionaires.

More important, aiming to abolish billionaires would involve reshaping the structure of the digital economy so that it produces a more equitable ratio of superrich to the rest of us.

Inequality is the defining economic condition of the tech age. Software, by its very nature, drives concentrations of wealth. Through network effects, in which the very popularity of a service ensures that it keeps getting more popular, and unprecedented economies of scale — in which Amazon can make Alexa once and have it work everywhere, for everyone — tech instills a winner-take-all dynamic across much of the economy.

We're already seeing these effects now. A few superstar corporations, many in tech, account for the bulk of American corporate profits, while most of the share of economic growth since the 1970s has gone to a small number of the country's richest people.

But the problem is poised to get worse. Artificial intelligence is creating prosperous new industries that don't employ very many workers; left unchecked, technology is creating a world where a few billionaires control an unprecedented share of global wealth.

But abolishment does not involve only economic policy. It might also take the form of social and political opprobrium. For at least 20 years, we've been in a devastating national love affair with billionaires — a dalliance that the tech industry has championed more than any other.

I've witnessed a generation of striving entrepreneurs join the three-comma club and instantly transform into superheroes of the global order, celebrated from the Bay Area to Beijing for what's taken to be their obvious and irrefutable wisdom about anything and everything. We put billionaires on magazine covers, speculate about their political ambitions, praise their grand visions to save the world and wink affectionately at their wacky plans to help us escape — thanks to their very huge and not-in-any-way-Freudianly-suggestive rockets — to a new one.

But the adulation we heap upon billionaires obscures the plain moral quandary at the center of their wealth: Why should anyone have a billion dollars, why should anyone be proud to brandish their billions, when there is so much suffering in the world?

As Ms. Ocasio-Cortez put it in a conversation with Ta-Nehisi Coates: "I'm not saying that Bill Gates or Warren Buffett are immoral, but a system that allows billionaires to exist when there are parts of

Alabama where people are still getting ringworm because they don't have access to public health is wrong." (She meant hookworm, she later corrected.)

Last week, to dig into this question of whether it was possible to be a good billionaire, I called up two experts.

The first was Peter Singer, the Princeton moral philosopher who has written extensively about the ethical duties of the rich. Mr. Singer told me that in general, he did not think it was possible to live morally as a billionaire, though he made a few exceptions: Mr. Gates and Mr. Buffett, who have pledged to give away the bulk of their wealth to philanthropy, would not earn Mr. Singer's scorn.

But most billionaires are not so generous; of the 2,200 or so billionaires in the world — about 500 of whom are American — fewer than 200 have signed the Giving Pledge created by Bill and Melinda Gates and Mr. Buffett.

"I have a moral concern with the conduct of individuals — we have many billionaires who are not living ethically, and are not doing nearly as much good as they can, by a wide margin," Mr. Singer said.

Then there is the additional complication of whether even the ones who are "doing good" are actually doing good. As the writer Anand Giridharadas has argued, many billionaires approach philanthropy as a kind of branding exercise to maintain a system in which they get to keep their billions.

When a billionaire commits to putting money into politics — whether it's Howard Schultz or Michael Bloomberg or Sheldon Adelson, whether it's for your team or the other — you should see the plan for what it is: an effort to gain some leverage over the political system, a scheme to short-circuit the revolution and blunt the advancing pitchforks.

Which brings me to my second expert on the subject, Tom Steyer, the former hedge-fund investor who is devoting his billion-dollar fortune to a passel of progressive causes, like voter registration and climate change and impeaching Donald Trump.

Mr. Steyer ticks every liberal box. He favors a wealth tax, and he and his wife have signed the Giving Pledge. He doesn't live excessively lavishly — he drives a Chevy Volt. Still, I wondered when I got on the phone with him last week: Wouldn't we be better off if we didn't have to worry about rich people like him trying to alter the political process?

Mr. Steyer was affable and loquacious; he spoke to me for nearly an hour about his interest in economic justice and his belief in grass-roots organizing. At one point I compared his giving with that of the Koch brothers, and he seemed genuinely pained by the comparison.

"I understand about the real issues of money in politics," he said. "We have a system that I know is not right, but it's the one we got, and we're trying as hard as possible to change it."

I admire his zeal. But if we tolerate the supposedly "good" billionaires in politics, we inevitably leave open the door for the bad ones. And the bad ones will overrun us. When American capitalism sends us its billionaires, it's not sending its best. It's sending us people who have lots of problems, and they're bringing those problems with them. They're bringing inequality. They're bringing injustice. They're buying politicians.

And some, I assume, are good people.

FARHAD MANJOO became an opinion columnist for The Times in 2018. Before that, he wrote the State of the Art column. He is the author of "True Enough: Learning to Live in a Post-Fact Society."

Don't Abolish Billionaires

OPINION | BY WILL WILKINSON | FEB. 21, 2019

Abolish bad policy instead.

BILLIONAIRES ARE IN notably bad odor with many people on the left. Socialists have long held that large stores of private wealth are tantamount to violence against those in need. But regular nonradical folks not on the left are fed up, too. Howard Schultz's potential independent White House bid is simply infuriating, and it's maddening to feel helplessly tangled in the gilded web of global intrigue emanating from the president, his plutocrat dictator pals and America's retail overlord, the philandering Jeff Bezos.

Thanks at least in part to Bernie Sanders and the sizzling rise of Alexandria Ocasio-Cortez, this dry wick has met a spark. Enthusiasm for radical leveling is whistling out of the hard-left fringe and blossoming into a mainstream mood.

Ms. Ocasio-Cortez's policy adviser, Dan Riffle, contends that "every billionaire is a policy failure" (that's the tagline on his Twitter handle) because "the acquisition of that much wealth has bad consequences" and "a moral society needs guardrails against it." He'd like to see the 2020 Democratic primary contenders answer a question: Can it be morally appropriate for anyone to be a billionaire?

It's a compelling litmus test. I'd also like to watch would-be Democratic nominees take it. However, I hope that they would stick up for the idea that it can be morally kosher to bank a billion and that the existence of virtuous three-comma fortunes is a sign not of failure but of supreme policy success.

The empirical record is quite clear about the general form of national political economy that produces the happiest, healthiest, wealthiest, freest and longest lives. There's no pithy name for it, so we'll have to settle for "liberal-democratic welfare-state capitalism." There's a "social democratic" version, which is what you get in countries like

Sweden, Norway and the Netherlands. And there's a "neoliberal" (usually English-speaking) version, which is what you get in countries like Canada, New Zealand and the United States.

You may prefer one version over the other, but they're not all that different. And in comparative terms, they're all insanely great. The typical citizen of these countries is as well-off as human beings have ever been. These places are the historical pinnacle of policy success.

But guess what? There are billionaires in all of them. Egalitarian Sweden, an object of ardent progressive adoration, has more billionaires per capita than the United States.

So what's the problem? Preventing billion-dollar hoards guards against the bad consequences of ... having the best sort of polity that has ever existed? The progressive idea here is usually that people with vastly more wealth than the common run of citizens wield vastly disproportionate political power and therefore imperil democracy and the equal worth of our basic rights. It's a worry we've got to take seriously, but it's based more in abstract theorizing than empirical analysis. Inspect any credible international ranking of countries by democratic quality, equal treatment under the law or level of personal freedom. You'll find the same passel of billionaire-tolerant states again and again. If there are billionaires in all the places where people flourish best, why think getting rid of them will make things go better?

It can be tempting to think that there's no morally decent way to accumulate *that* much wealth. And it's true that scads of the filthy rich got that way through theft, exploitation and the subtler corruption of anti-competitive rules in politically rigged markets. (You may have heard of Donald Trump.)

But there's a big moral difference between positive-sum wealth production and zero-sum wealth extraction — a difference that corresponds to a rough-and-ready distinction between the deserving and undeserving rich. The distinction is sound because there's a proven way to make a moral killing: improve a huge number of other people's lives while capturing a tiny slice of the surplus value.

Consider Dr. Gary Michelson, a spinal surgeon and inventor worth an estimated $1.8 billion. He lives in Los Angeles. Dr. Michelson holds hundreds of patents on medical devices and procedures that have made spinal surgery more effective. He got rich by making it so that people with spinal injuries could walk again or suffer less debilitating pain.

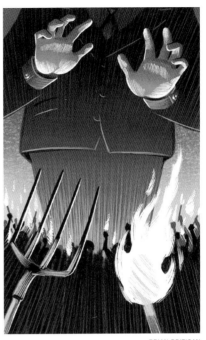

BRIAN BRITIGAN

According to William Nordhaus, the Nobel Prize-winning economist, innovators capture about 2 percent of the economic value they create. The rest of it accrues to consumers. Whatever that is, it's not a raw deal. The accumulation of these innovations over time is the mechanism that drives compounding economic growth, which accounts for a vast improvement over the past 100 years in the typical American standard of living. Some people may have made an ungodly sum in the course of helping make this humanitarian miracle happen, but that's O.K.

This isn't to say that the deserving rich deserve every penny they get. In a better world, billionaires like Dr. Michelson would probably have less. Policy failure is rife, and it's bound to account for a portion of even the best-deserved fortunes. Patents, for example, are government-granted monopolies meant to incentivize innovation. But the evidence suggests we've overshot the mark, and the pace of innovation would quicken, and many of America's biggest fortunes would shrink, if patent protections were weakened.

Along similar lines, few of us object to J.K. Rowling making a mint entertaining billions of kids (and adults), but much of her net worth is because of merchandising profits built on unjustifiably ironclad intellectual property rights, which have deprived billions of the joys of knockoff Harry Potter toys and stories. Nearly every real-world market is defined to some extent by rules that limit competition, concentrate wealth and leave the rest of us poorer than we might have been. A small number of people have too much housing wealth because we've made it too hard to build. Financial innovation makes new markets and improves the allocation of resources, but Wall Street tycoons also reap huge rewards from winning wasteful arbitrage arms races, skimming off transactions and nickel-and-diming consumers with inscrutable fees.

Fixing these policy failures might create a system that produces fewer billionaires. But that shouldn't be the point. It might also produce more morally worthy 10-figure fortunes. That's great, because we should be aiming to channel entrepreneurial energy into productive wealth creation that lifts us all up and away from the extraction of wealth through unjust rules that close off opportunity and deprive us of the blessings of innovation.

There is a possible America where routes to extractive wealth have been closed and barriers to productive wealth have been cleared; where the wealthiest have somewhat less, and the rest of us have a great deal more. In this America, our economy and democracy are more equitable and less corrupt, and the least well-off fare better than ever. We should dearly want to live there, in a place where, if you can manage to become one, it's more than "morally appropriate" to be a billionaire.

WILL WILKINSON is a contributing opinion writer and the vice president for research at the Niskanen Center.

Who Gets to Own the West?

BY JULIE TURKEWITZ | JUNE 22, 2019

A new group of billionaires is shaking up the landscape.

IDAHO CITY, IDAHO — The Wilks brothers grew up in a goat shed, never finished high school and built a billion-dollar fracking business from scratch.

So when the brothers, Dan and Farris, bought a vast stretch of mountain-studded land in southwest Idaho, it was not just an investment, but a sign of their good fortune.

"Through hard work and determination — and they didn't have a lot of privilege — they've reached success," said Dan Wilks's son, Justin.

The purchase also placed the Wilkses high on the list of well-heeled landowners who are buying huge parcels of America. In the last decade, private land in the United States has become increasingly concentrated in the hands of a few. Today, just 100 families own about 42 million acres across the country, a 65,000-square-mile expanse, according to the Land Report, a magazine that tracks large purchases. Researchers at the magazine have found that the amount of land owned by those 100 families has jumped 50 percent since 2007.

Much of that land stretches from the Rocky Mountains down into Texas, where, for some, commercial forests and retired ranches have become an increasingly attractive investment.

Battles over private and public land have been a defining part of the West since the 1800s, when the federal government began doling out free acres to encourage expansion. For years, fights have played out between private individuals and the federal government, which owns more than half of the region.

But now, with wealthier buyers purchasing even larger parcels, the battle lines have shifted. Many local residents see these new owners as a threat to a way of life beloved for its easy access to the outdoors,

Payette River canyon in Smiths Ferry, Idaho. Parts of the area are now owned by Dan and Farris Wilks, leaders among a new class of landowners who are buying up vast parcels of the West.

and they complain that property that they once saw as public is being taken away from them.

The Wilkses, who now own some 700,000 acres across several states, have become a symbol of the out-of-touch owner. In Idaho, as their property has expanded, the brothers have shuttered trails and hired armed guards to patrol their acres, blocking and stymying access not only to their private property, but also to some publicly owned areas. This has drawn ire from everyday Idahoans who have hiked and hunted in those hills for generations.

The Wilks brothers see what they are doing as a duty. God had given them much, Justin said. In return, he said, "we feel that we have a responsibility to the land."

Some of the new owners have been welcomed. The cable magnate, John Malone, for instance, has been praised by the Nature Conservancy for his family's conservation efforts, and other buyers have helped to clean up trails and restore pristine acres.

The arrival of this new class of landholders comes as the region is experiencing the fastest population boom in the country, which is driving up housing prices and the cost of living and leaving many residents fearful of losing their culture and economic stability.

In Idaho, Rocky Barker, a retired columnist for The Idaho Statesman, has called the conflict a "clash between two American dreams," pitting the nation's respect for private property rights against the notion of a beauty-rich public estate set aside for the enjoyment of all.

The clash, he said, is part of a larger transformation of the region — from an economy rooted in extraction to one based on recreation; from a working class culture to a more moneyed one. "Big landowners," he said, "are just another new force."

THE GATE

Tim Horting is among the people caught up in the debate. Mr. Horting, 58, a heavy equipment salesman, grew up hiking in the woods north of Boise, a forest threaded by dirt routes that offer views of the state's celebrated peaks. He learned the terrain from his father, who taught him to chop wood, gut deer and haul game home for dinner.

Mr. Horting and his wife, Kim, built a cabin in those woods in 2006, right by Boise Ridge Road, which led to a popular recreation area built mostly on public land. The Hortings said they wanted their grandchildren to grow up with a feel for rural life. "This is the whole reason I moved here," Mr. Horting said. For years, he assumed the road was public, and he would guide his ATV up its steep ascent, his grandchildren in tow.

A generation of hikers, hunters and snowmobilers had done the same.

Then, in 2016, the Wilkses purchased 172,000 acres at the edge of Mr. Horting's home. Soon, a gate went up on the road, and a sign was tacked to a nearby tree: "Warning. Private Property. No Trespassing."

To Mr. Horting and others, Boise Ridge Road was now closed.

It was just the beginning. Gates with "private property" signs were going up across the region. In some places, the Wilkses' road closings were legal. In other cases, it wasn't clear. Road law is a tangled knot, and Boise County had little money to grapple with it in court. So the gates stayed up.

The problem, said Mr. Horting, "is not the fact that they own the property. It's that they've cut off public roads."

"We're being bullied," he added. "We can't compete and they know it."

THE OWNERS

In recent years, longtime timber and fossil fuel investors have been joined by newer types of buyers in the region.

Brokers say the new arrivals are driven in part by a desire to invest in natural assets while they are still abundant, particularly amid a fear of economic, political and climate volatility.

"There is a tremendous underground, not-so-subtle awareness from people who realize that resources are getting scarcer and scarcer," said Bernard Uechtritz, a real estate adviser.

Among the nation's top landowners are Mr. Malone, with 2.2 million acres in New Mexico, Colorado and other states; the media mogul Ted Turner, with two million acres in Montana, Nebraska and elsewhere; Peter Buck, a founder of Subway; Charles and David Koch, who run cattle outside of Lubbock, Tex.; and Jeff Bezos, who operates his space company from a West Texas outpost. William Bruce Harrison, the scion to an oil fortune, now owns 19 mountains in Colorado.

In the intermountain West, the purchases come amid a population boom that has exacerbated local concerns about the loss of space and culture. Last year, Idaho and Nevada were the fastest growing states in the nation, followed closely by Utah, Arizona and Colorado.

These new buyers have become a symbol of a bigger problem: The gentrification of the interior West.

In 2018, more than 20,000 Californians arrived in Idaho; home prices around Boise also jumped 17 percent. This has meant not just new subdivisions and microbreweries, but also packed schools, crowded ski trails and heightened anxiety among teachers, plumbers and others, who are finding that they can no longer afford a first home.

When Stan Kroenke, the owner of the Los Angeles Rams, purchased a vast Texas ranch in 2016, he sent eviction notices to dozens of people with homes around a lake, some of whom were retirees with little money for a move. At the time, his representatives said he was returning the shoreline to a more natural state.

THE WILKSES

The Wilks brothers, the sons of a bricklayer, grew up outside Cisco, Tex., a town of fewer than 4,000 people where their father was the head of a conservative church called the Assembly of Yahweh.

At first, the brothers founded a masonry company. In 2001, seeing a business opportunity, they began building fracking equipment, just as an oil-and-gas boom took off. A decade later, they sold Frac Tech for a reported $3.5 billion.

This has allowed them to donate generously to causes they believe in, including right-wing media outlets, Senator Ted Cruz's White House run and President Trump's re-election bid. It has also allowed them to buy enormous parcels, particularly in Montana, where they are prolific donors to local politicians, and in Idaho, where they've hired lobbyists to protect their interests.

In Montana, they own some 300,000 acres, and have built several homes and a private airport on a property called N Bar ranch. Today, they live mostly in Texas.

Justin Wilks said they had shuttered their Idaho acres to protect them, after years of unchecked snowmobiling and camping had ruined much of the landscape.

"We want to be good neighbors," Mr. Wilks said. "I know some people think we haven't been, just because we haven't let them freely roam across our property as they saw fit. But I'll also offer: Do you want me camping in your front yard?"

CONSERVATION

The concept of private property is embedded in the nation's framework, and many large landowners cite this as the foundation for their holdings.

"John earned everything that he's made," said Rye Austin, who leads the land preservation foundation created by John Malone's family. "If he wants to purchase and own land, we live in a capitalist country, why shouldn't someone be able to buy land? That's the whole concept of private property."

Many landowners are engaged in conservation and have entered into easements that limit future development on their parcels, and also provide them with significant tax breaks.

But setting aside land for conservation has not always staved off criticism.

In Idaho, the Wilks brothers did more than gate a few roads. They also revoked road-use contracts that propped up the region's multimillion-dollar snowmobile industry, shut down hunting on their land and told timber companies to pull crews from the area. About 100 people lost their jobs.

No one claimed that those actions were illegal, but they heightened fears that local residents were losing control of the region. A 2017 video of a roadside argument between an armed Wilks guard and a local ATV rider traveled quickly around the state.

Afterward, the Wilks family hired a lobbyist to push for a law that would stiffen penalties for trespass. The bill passed.

Amid the dispute, some residents emailed the Wilkses, asking permission to cross their property. They were surprised to receive a response suggesting they first visit a popular right-wing website and share their opinions of its content.

The site, PragerU, features videos supporting the hard-lined conservative views of personalities like Ben Shapiro and Dinesh D'Souza. The portal has been heavily financed by the Wilkses.

Mr. Horting, a lifelong conservative, was "insulted," he said. "I'm not going to give my political views to use your land."

Soon, the brothers were the subject of articles in The Idaho Statesman. County prosecutors began investigating the road closings and explored litigation.

In a series of peace offerings, the brothers reopened access to some snowmobile trails and restarted some logging. More recently, they opened the gate on Boise Ridge Road and removed the No Trespass signs. Some people in the area, including the Valley County recreation director, Larry Laxson, applauded the effort. "They did a lot of things wrong when they came to Valley County," he said, "but it's getting better."

Mr. Wilks said he was trying to resolve access issues with frustrated neighbors. But ultimately, he said, "our Heavenly Father has blessed us with lots of gifts," and his family's priority was to protect them.

DORIS BURKE and **ALAIN DELAQUÉRIÈRE** contributed research.

JULIE TURKEWITZ is a national correspondent based in Denver. Since joining the Times in 2014, she has driven more than 200,000 miles around the country, writing about a variety of issues and covering disasters such as hurricanes and wildfires.

A Message From the Billionaire's Club: Tax Us

BY PATRICIA COHEN | JUNE 24, 2019

ENTHUSIASM FOR A WEALTH TAX on the country's thin sliver of multimillionaires and billionaires may be unsurprising — after all, most Americans wouldn't have to pay it. But now the idea is attracting support from a handful of those who would.

A letter published Monday on the website Medium.com calls for "a moderate wealth tax on the fortunes of the richest one-tenth of the richest 1 percent of Americans — on us."

The "us" includes self-made billionaires like the financier George Soros and Chris Hughes, a Facebook co-founder, as well as heirs to dynastic riches like the filmmaker Abigail Disney and Liesel Pritzker Simmons and Ian Simmons, co-founders of the Blue Haven Initiative, an impact investment organization.

"We thought it would be a good idea," Mr. Simmons explained by phone as he waited out a traffic jam in the Boston area. "Liesel and I decided to reach out to some other folks to see if they thought it was a good idea, too."

The letter came together in the last two weeks. Eighteen individuals, spread among 11 families, added their names. All are active in progressive research and political organizations, some of which are pointedly focused on the swelling gap between the richest Americans and everyone else.

A recent analysis of a Federal Reserve report found that over the last three decades, the wealthiest 1 percent of Americans saw their net worth grow by $21 trillion, while the wealth of the bottom 50 percent fell by $900 billion.

The letter is addressed to all presidential contenders, and refers specifically to a plan offered by Senator Elizabeth Warren of Massachusetts. Her proposal would create a wealth tax for households with

$50 million or more in assets — including stocks, bonds, yachts, cars and art. She estimates such a tax would affect 75,000 families, and raise $2.75 trillion over 10 years.

A desire to curb the rising concentration of wealth has long been part of the Democrats' core message, but a Republican tax bill in 2017 that delivered the biggest benefits to Americans with the highest incomes reinvigorated the debate.

In recent months, Democrats including Representative Alexandria Ocasio-Cortez of New York and Senator Bernie Sanders of Vermont have offered up ambitious tax proposals targeted at wealthy taxpayers. At the same time, they have questioned whether vast family fortunes conferring outsize economic and political power are inimical to democratic values.

Surveys undertaken in the wake of those proposals showed that roughly seven out of 10 Americans supported higher taxes on the wealthiest Americans.

The swirl of attention provided an opportunity to advance the conversation around inequality, social responsibility and taxes, Mr. Hughes said.

"One thing that we collectively want to see is further research and more activism on policy design," he added. His husband, Sean Eldridge, a founder of the progressive advocacy group Stand Up America and a former congressional candidate, also signed the letter.

The letter unequivocally declares that a wealth tax "strengthens American freedom and democracy" and "is patriotic."

And it points out that economic researchers estimate that the richest 0.1 percent of Americans will pay 3.2 percent of their wealth in taxes this year compared with 7.2 percent paid by the bottom 99 percent. "The next dollar of new tax revenue should come from the most financially fortunate, not from middle-income and lower-income Americans," the letter declares.

Ms. Simmons said a wealth tax could help deal with problems like the "lack of child care, educational debt, the opioid crisis and the climate crisis."

She is part of the Pritzker family, the founders of one of the country's largest private companies, which included the Hyatt hotel chain. Another family member, Regan Pritzker, president of the San Francisco-based Libra Foundation, also signed.

Members of the billionaire club have previously argued that they should be taxed more. In 2011, Warren E. Buffett, the founder of Berkshire Hathaway, published an essay noting that his effective tax rate was "actually a lower percentage than was paid by any of the other 20 people in our office." His comments prompted President Barack Obama and others to push for a "Buffett rule" mandating that millionaires pay at least 30 percent of their income in taxes.

In 2014, Nick Hanauer, a Seattle-based entrepreneur, published a memo to "My Fellow Zillionaires" noting that "people like you and me are thriving beyond the dreams of any plutocrats in history, the rest of the country — the 99.99 percent — is lagging far behind."

He added: "If we don't do something to fix the glaring inequities in this economy, the pitchforks are going to come for us."

Mr. Hanauer signed the letter published on Monday, as did Molly Munger, a lawyer whose father is Charlie Munger, vice chairman of Berkshire Hathaway. She and her husband, Stephen English, were co-founders of the Advancement Project, a civil rights organization. He also signed the letter.

Other names on the letter were Stephen M. Silberstein, co-founder of the software company Innovative Interfaces; the philanthropist and arts patron Agnes Gund and her daughter Catherine Gund, the founder and director of Aubin Pictures; Arnold S. Hiatt, chairman of the Stride Rite Charitable Foundation; Justin Rosenstein, a co-founder of Asana, which provides work-management tools; Robert S. Bowditch Jr., the founder of MB Associates, a real estate development firm, and his wife, Louise; and Mr. Soros's son Alexander, deputy chair of the Open Society Foundations.

The final signatory was "Anonymous."

The Rich Really Do Pay Lower Taxes Than You

OPINION | BY DAVID LEONHARDT | OCT. 6, 2019

ALMOST A DECADE AGO, Warren Buffett made a claim that would become famous. He said that he paid a lower tax rate than his secretary, thanks to the many loopholes and deductions that benefit the wealthy.

His claim sparked a debate about the fairness of the tax system. In the end, the expert consensus was that, whatever Buffett's specific situation, most wealthy Americans did not actually pay a lower tax rate than the middle class. "Is it the norm?" the fact-checking outfit Politifact asked. "No."

Time for an update: It's the norm now.

For the first time on record, the 400 wealthiest Americans last year paid a lower total tax rate — spanning federal, state and local taxes — than any other income group, according to newly released data.

That's a sharp change from the 1950s and 1960s, when the wealthy paid vastly higher tax rates than the middle class or poor.

Since then, taxes that hit the wealthiest the hardest — like the estate tax and corporate tax — have plummeted, while tax avoidance has become more common.

President Trump's 2017 tax cut, which was largely a handout to the rich, plays a role, too. It helped push the tax rate on the 400 wealthiest households below the rates for almost everyone else.

The overall tax rate on the richest 400 households last year was only 23 percent, meaning that their combined tax payments equaled less than one quarter of their total income. This overall rate was 70 percent in 1950 and 47 percent in 1980.

For middle-class and poor families, the picture is different. Federal income taxes have also declined modestly for these families, but they haven't benefited much if at all from the decline in the corporate tax or estate tax. And they now pay more in payroll taxes (which finance

Medicare and Social Security) than in the past. Over all, their taxes have remained fairly flat.

The combined result is that over the last 75 years the United States tax system has become radically less progressive.

The data here come from the most important book on government policy that I've read in a long time — called "The Triumph of Injustice," to be released next week. The authors are Emmanuel Saez and Gabriel Zucman, both professors at the University of California, Berkeley, who have done pathbreaking work on taxes. Saez has won the award that goes to the top academic economist under age 40, and Zucman was recently profiled on the cover of Bloomberg BusinessWeek magazine as "the wealth detective."

They have constructed a historical database that tracks the tax payments of households at different points along the income spectrum going back to 1913, when the federal income tax began. The story they tell is maddening — and yet ultimately energizing.

"Many people have the view that nothing can be done," Zucman told me. "Our case is, 'No, that's wrong. Look at history.' " As they write in the book: "Societies can choose whatever level of tax progressivity they want." When the United States has raised tax rates on the wealthy and made rigorous efforts to collect those taxes, it has succeeded in doing so.

And it can succeed again.

Saez and Zucman portray the history of American taxes as a struggle between people who want to tax the rich and those who want to protect the fortunes of the rich. The story starts in the 17th century, when Northern colonies created more progressive tax systems than Europe had. Massachusetts even enacted a wealth tax, which covered financial holdings, land, ships, jewelry, livestock and more.

The Southern colonies, by contrast, were hostile to taxation. Plantation owners worried that taxes could undermine slavery by eroding the wealth of shareholders, as the historian Robin Einhorn has explained, and made sure to keep tax rates low and tax collection ineffective. (The Confederacy's hostility to taxes ultimately hampered its ability to raise money and fight the Civil War.)

By the middle of the 20th century, the high-tax advocates had prevailed. The United States had arguably the world's most progressive tax code, with a top income-tax rate of 91 percent and a corporate tax rate above 50 percent.

But the second half of the 20th century was mostly a victory for the low-tax side. Companies found ways to take more deductions and dodge taxes. Politicians cut every tax that fell heavily on the wealthy: high-end income taxes, investment taxes, the estate tax and the corporate tax. The justification for doing so was usually that the economy as a whole would benefit.

The justification turned out to be wrong. The wealthy, and only the wealthy, have done fantastically well over the last several decades. G.D.P. growth has been disappointing, and middle-class income growth even worse.

The American economy just doesn't function very well when tax rates on the rich are low and inequality is sky high. It was true in the lead-up to the Great Depression, and it's been true recently. Which means that raising high-end taxes isn't about punishing the rich (who, by the way, will still be rich). It's about creating an economy that works better for the vast majority of Americans.

In their book, Saez and Zucman sketch out a modern progressive tax code. The overall tax rate on the richest 1 percent would roughly double, to about 60 percent. The tax increases would bring in about $750 billion a year, or 4 percent of G.D.P., enough to pay for universal pre-K, an infrastructure program, medical research, clean energy and more. Those are the kinds of policies that do lift economic growth.

One crucial part of the agenda is a minimum global corporate tax of at least 25 percent. A company would have to pay the tax on its profits in the United States even if it set up headquarters in Ireland or Bermuda. Saez and Zucman also favor a wealth tax; Elizabeth Warren's version is based on their work. And they call for the creation of a Public Protection Bureau, to help the I.R.S. crack down on tax dodging.

I already know what some critics will say about these arguments — that the rich will always figure out a way to avoid taxes. That's simply not the case. True, they will always manage to avoid some taxes. But history shows that serious attempts to collect more taxes usually succeed.

Ask yourself this: If efforts to tax the superrich were really doomed to fail, why would so many of the superrich be fighting so hard to defeat those efforts?

DAVID LEONHARDT is a former Washington bureau chief for the Times, and was the founding editor of The Upshot and head of The 2020 Project, on the future of the Times newsroom. He won the 2011 Pulitzer Prize for commentary, for columns on the financial crisis.

Why Don't Rich People Just Stop Working?

BY ALEX WILLIAMS

PUBLISHED OCT. 17, 2019 | UPDATED OCT. 18, 2019

Are the wealthy addicted to money, competition, or just feeling important? Yes.

"BILLIONAIRES SHOULD NOT EXIST," Senator Bernie Sanders said last month. And, at the Democratic presidential debate this week, he said that the wealth disparity in America is "a moral and economic outrage."

"Senator Sanders is right," said Tom Steyer, a businessman from California who happened to be the only billionaire onstage that night (as far as we know).

"No one on this stage wants to protect billionaires — not even the billionaire wants to protect billionaires," noted Senator Amy Klobuchar.

It's an idea that's going around. Mark Zuckerberg, the Facebook founder who is worth close to $70 billion, is apparently open to it. "I don't know that I have an exact threshold on what amount of money someone should have," he said in live-streamed question-and-answer session with company employees in early October. "But on some level, no one deserves to have that much money."

Yet here we are, chugging into the 10th year of an extremely top-heavy economic boom in which the 1 percenters, by all statistical measures, have won, creating the greatest wealth disparity since the Jazz Age. This era, in length and gains, dwarfs the "greed is good" 1980s, that era of yellow ties, nigiri rolls and designer espresso machines that has come to symbolize gilded excess in popular imagination.

And yet the only thing we know in this casino-like economy — a casino that may, in fact, soon be shuttered — is that for those at the top, too much is never enough.

Many normal, non-billionaire people wonder: why is that?

Studies over the years have indicated that the rich, unlike the leisured gentry of old, tend to work longer hours and spend less time

Mark Zuckerberg speaking at the Facebook F8 conference in 2017.

socializing. Tim Cook, the chief executive of Apple, whose worth has been estimated in the hundreds of millions, has said that he wakes up at 3:45 a.m. to mount his daily assault on his corporate rivals. Elon Musk, the man behind Tesla and SpaceX, is worth some $23 billion but nevertheless considers it a victory that he dialed back his "bonkers" 120-hour workweeks to a more "manageable" 80 or 90.

And they continue to diversify. Lady Gaga makes a reported $1 million per show in her residency at the Park MGM in Las Vegas, and has evolved from pop music to conquer film — but still also recently unveiled a cosmetics venture with Amazon.

Almost everything rich people touch makes money, but this current financial inferno has meant little for the bottom 50 percent of earners in the United States, who have 32 percent less wealth than they did in 2003.

The 1 percent have, as of last decade, 85 percent of their net worth tied up in investments like stocks, bonds and private equity, where value has exploded. According to Redfin, the average sale price of properties in the top 5 percent are up 43 percent nationally over the past decade, and up even more in Los Angeles and San Francisco.

Fine vintage watches, which have become a must-have for the young male money class, are exploding in value, with prices on certain five-figure models of Rolexes doubling in just a few years.

Gold, once derided as a relic, is up 40 percent in the past few years. What's happening?

NO ONE HAS A RETIREMENT NUMBER THESE DAYS

"What's your number?" asked anyone caught up in the dot-com boom of the 1990s.

Could you retire to Napa with $5 million? $20 million?

Some hit their number and some went bust, but Silicon Valley is more than ever a showcase for the unfettered capitalism of 2019.

Yet no one seems to talk about their number anymore, said Antonio García Martínez, who sold a start-up to Twitter and served as a Facebook product manager before publishing his memoir, "Chaos Monkeys: Obscene Fortune and Random Failure in Silicon Valley," in 2016.

Yesterday's big score is just seed capital for tomorrow's bigger one.

"There's never some omega point," Mr. García Martínez, 43, said. "People who get to that point don't stop once they get there."

"People say, 'Why don't you develop a hobby, or do philanthropy?' " Mr. García Martínez said. "But for many, they simply can't stop doing it. They derive transcendent meaning from capitalism. Without their money, what else would they have?"

At a time of low taxes, friendly interest rates and torrents of venture capital available to would-be moguls, it's a historic moment in the quest for more among the entrepreneurial class.

Tim Ferriss, the life-hacking author and podcast star who was an angel investor in Silicon Valley for nearly a decade, wrote in an email that many of these people have been "navigating work and life in sixth gear for decades."

WITHOUT CONSTANT WORK, WE MUST FACE THE NATURE OF EXISTENCE

"Once they have no financial need to work — are 'post-economic,' as some say in San Francisco — they have trouble shifting into lower gears," Mr. Ferriss wrote. "They're like drag racers who now have to learn to navigate the turns and intersections of neighborhoods at 30 miles per hour."

"Without ambitious projects to fill space," he added, "there is often a void that makes some of the bigger questions hard to avoid. The things you neglected are no longer drowned out by noise; they are the signal. It's like facing the Ghost of Christmas Past."

In a sense, it has been going on in this country for two and a half centuries. "We are a nation founded on the overthrow of kings and the idle rich, so the hustle is deeply baked into mainstream notions of what it means to be American," said Margaret O'Mara, a history professor at the University of Washington who is a New York Times opinion contributor.

And today's competitive personality types are unable to slow down, in part because they fear slipping from their lofty perches.

"Driven people are just driven," said Maria Bartiromo, the Fox Business anchor. "They want to stay fresh and relevant, and to do that, it requires consistent practice. If you want to win, you need to be all in." And winning can be collecting the most cash — pressing the excitement pedal over and over again, like so many exhausted rats in a cage.

RICH PEOPLE KNOW TOO MANY RICH PEOPLE

With the number of Americans making $1 million or more spiking by 40 percent between 2010 and 2016, according to the Internal Revenue Service, you may think that the rich are finally feeling flush enough to ease up, kick back, chill out.

They are not.

One recent Harvard survey of 4,000 millionaires found that people worth $8 million or more were scarcely happier than those worth $1 million.

In a widely cited 2006 study, rich people reported that they spend more time doing things they were required to do.

Why do they want to do this to themselves?

The fact that there are more rich people who are, in fact, richer than ever may be part of the reason.

Sociologists have long talked about "relative income hypothesis." We tend to measure material satisfaction by those around us — not in absolute terms.

"For most people, enough is enough," said Robert Frank, the wealth editor for CNBC and the author of the 2007 book "Richistan: A Journey Through the American Wealth Boom and the Lives of the New Rich," who has interviewed many plutocrats. "But there is another group of people, no matter what they have, they have to keep going. I call them 'scorekeepers.' They're truly driven by competitive zeal."

Take Larry Ellison, the billionaire co-founder of Oracle. Mr. Ellison always felt competitive with Bill Gates and Paul Allen of Microsoft, Mr. Frank said. "So when Paul Allen built his 400-foot boat, Larry Ellison waited until it was done and built a 450-foot boat. Larry Ellison would never be happy until he was No. 1."

Among the very rich, it does not matter that all imaginable material needs have been met, said Edward Wolff, a professor of economics at New York University who studies wealth and disparity.

"Among the rarefied group of the extreme rich, social status depends on net worth," Dr. Wolff wrote in an email. "Their enhanced wealth allows them to make substantial charitable contributions to institutions like museums and concert halls, that may lead to having a building or the like named after them. Think of the Koch brothers and the New York City Ballet. This is only possible if they can stay ahead of the pack and out-contribute their peers."

Social sampling leads the rich toward a blinkered view that society as a whole is more well-off than it is, feeding their unending need — particularly as wealth becomes geographically dense. Nearly 20 percent of the world's ultra-high-net-worth individuals — with assets of

$30 million or more — live in just 10 cities around the globe, by one tally. Six of those cities are in the United States.

MONEY IS LIKE ALCOHOL BUT FOR MONEY

Living inside bubbles, the rich need greater excess just to feel the same high, said Steven Berglas, a psychologist, executive coach and author.

"If you're an alcoholic," he said, "you're going to take one drink, two drinks, five drinks, six drinks to feel the buzz. Well, when you get a million dollars, you need 10 million dollars to feel like a king. Money is an addictive substance."

Feeding the addiction becomes even more challenging in a top-heavy economy where the price tags of the status symbols keep adding zeros.

For the superrich looking to buy their way in to professional sports, it's no longer enough to have courtside seats or a luxury box. You need a team. They're pricey.

The Golden State Warriors, for example, sold in 2010 for an N.B.A. record $450 million to an ownership group headed by Joe Lacob, a Silicon Valley venture capitalist. The team is now valued at $3.5 billion.

Even that is not enough. Now you have to build the biggest, flashiest arena. The Warriors owners recently put the finishing touches on a gleaming new waterfront arena in San Francisco called the Chase Center. It was financed largely by themselves for $1.4 billion.

Not to be left behind, Steve Ballmer, the former Microsoft chief and owner of the rival Los Angeles Clippers, is seeking to build a $1 billion pleasure dome of his own in Inglewood, Calif.

Clustered courtside together at the sporting palaces, the celebrities, naturally, begin to envy the fortunes of the moguls near them.

Even at the pinnacle of success, entertainers like Mark Wahlberg and Lady Gaga find themselves "suddenly in the same world with billionaires and financiers who own private jets and have their own boats," Mr. Frank said. "There's only so much you can make in entertainment, so they look around and decide that they need to get to the next level that they're encountering socially at the Met Ball and at charity functions."

The opportunity appears endless. But what if it's not?

THE RICH SUSPECT THE ROLLER COASTER IS ABOUT TO CRASH

As a hedge fund veteran, precious metals adviser and financial author, James Rickards is a rich guy who talks to a lot of other rich guys. They don't always like what he has to say.

He believes that the current debt-fueled recovery may be a prelude for an economic collapse to dwarf the Great Recession. Until recently, he said, such theories were met with polite lack of interest by many wealthy people. Lately, something has changed.

"Literally, in a matter of weeks, certainly a couple of months, the phone calls have had a different tone to them," Mr. Rickards said. "What I'm hearing is, 'I've got the money. How do I hang on to it?' 'Are gold futures going to hold up or should I have bullion?' 'If I have bullion, should I put it in a bag in a private vault?' "

"It's a level of concern that I've never heard from the superrich," he said. "The tone of voice is, 'I need an answer now!' "

It is not just the rockiness of the stock market. The fears of the wealthy seem to be of a more existential nature.

It is as if the very people who have profited most from these good times cannot believe that times are good — or that they will stay good, in the event of, say, a Bernie Sanders presidency.

Paul Singer, who oversees the behemoth Elliott Management fund, is reportedly tapping investors for billions as a war chest for a possible market implosion.

Among the tech zillionaire classes, a place to bug out in the event of an economic collapse, environmental disaster or violent uprising became the thing to have.

After he left Facebook, Mr. García Martínez himself bought five wooded acres on an island in the Pacific Northwest equipped with generators and solar panels, as The New Yorker reported in 2017.

When any part of the denial of rich people gets punctured, the boom reveals itself to be a very weird boom. The profits themselves are confusing. Even some who have ridden the wave to outsize fortunes see something amiss.

Marc Benioff, a chief executive of Salesforce.com, recently declared that "capitalism as we know it is dead." Corporate earnings are often tepid, yet stocks in those same companies are soaring, thanks in part to stock buybacks that fatten executive compensation but do little to help the business.

Some even notice the rest of us out here. Ray Dalio, the hedge fund billionaire, recently wrote an essay on LinkedIn that capitalism "is not working well for the majority of Americans because it's producing self-reinforcing spirals up for the haves and down for the have-nots."

And for those who amass fortunes, the money is the only measure of success they have, said Jordan Belfort, the real-life inspiration for "The Wolf of Wall Street."

As opposed to people who build businesses that make actual products, "a lot of Wall Street traders didn't create anything — all they did was trade on the value and ingenuity of what other people created, so at the end of the day, what can they point to that's tangible?" Mr. Belfort said. (He disavowed his former excess after a prison stint and became a motivational speaker.)

"All they have is money," he said. "So they go out and buy a house and a fancy car, and that feels good for a short while, then they buy a second house and a fancier car. Because all they have is what they earn. They're defined by it."

The newly rich from normal backgrounds are the most anxious of all, said Jennifer Streaks, a personal finance commentator and CNBC contributor.

"Imagine growing up middle class or even poor and then amassing millions," Ms. Streaks said. "This sounds like the American dream, but suddenly you have a $5 million apartment, a $200,000 car and a family that has these expectations."

A panic ensues when those people believe "that they are one bad investment away from being broke."

AND THE RICH BECOME ANXIOUS AND ISOLATED

It's not like Jeff Bezos, the $110 billion man, is going to have to auction off his $65 million Gulfstream jet if he makes a bad bet on Amazon delivery drones (or goes through a $36 billion divorce).

Even so, the isolation that often accompanies extreme wealth can provide an emotional impulse to keep on earning, long after material comforts have been met, said T. Byram Karasu, an emeritus professor of psychiatry at the Albert Einstein College of Medicine in the Bronx who said he has worked with numerous high earners in his private practice.

Apex entrepreneurs and financiers, after all, are often "adrenaline-fueled, transgressive people," Dr. Karasu said. "They tend to have laser-focused digital brains, are always in transactional mode, and the bigger they get, the lonelier they are, because they do not belong."

Dr. Berglas, a onetime member of the Harvard Medical School faculty in psychology, said: "If you can't relate to people, you presume that the failure to have rewarding relationships is because of jealousy — your house is three-X your neighbors', and they look at your brand-new Corvette and drool. It's a compensatory mechanism — 'I might not have a ton of friends, but I can do anything I want and I'm the most powerful S.O.B. there is.' "

Limitless opportunity, extreme isolation. They already own the present. What else is left to buy but tomorrow, and the tomorrow after that? Suddenly, the fetish of the superrich for space tourism starts to make sense.

CHAPTER 2

Billionaires in the Limelight: Jeff Bezos and Oprah Winfrey

While many billionaires conduct their lives out of the spotlight, there are a few who enter the celebrity class. Jeff Bezos, the founder of Amazon, whose extreme wealth, personal dramas and growing interest in Hollywood have attracted headlines, has become a household name. And Oprah Winfrey, who made her fortune as an entertainer, is perhaps one of the best known billionaires in America, as well as the only black woman on Forbes's list of America's wealthiest people.

Jeff Bezos Wants Ideas for Philanthropy, So He Asked Twitter

BY NICK WINGFIELD | JUNE 15, 2017

YOU'RE AN ASTRONOMICALLY wealthy tech mogul who has mastered the art of getting people to spend money with your company over the internet. How do you come up with fresh ideas for giving some of your fortune away?

If you're Jeff Bezos, the founder and chief executive of Amazon .com, you fire up Twitter, naturally.

On Thursday, Mr. Bezos sent a tweet to his more than 222,000 followers asking for suggestions for philanthropic giving. He specifically asked for ideas that could help the world in the near term, a contrast to long-term personal investments he has made in for-profit companies with social impact, like Blue Origin, a space firm, and The Washington Post.

Mr. Bezos wrote, "I'm thinking I want much of my philanthropic activity to be helping people in the here and now — short term — at the intersection of urgent need and lasting impact."

Request for ideas…

This tweet is a request for ideas. I'm thinking about a philanthropy strategy that is the opposite of how I mostly spend my time – working on the long term. For philanthropy, I find I'm drawn to the other end of the spectrum: the right now. As one example, I'm very inspired and moved by the work done at Mary's Place here in Seattle. I like long-term – it's a huge lever: Blue Origin, Amazon, Washington Post – all of these are contributing to society and civilization in their own ways. But I'm thinking I want much of my philanthropic activity to be helping people in the here and now – short term – at the intersection of urgent need and lasting impact. If you have ideas, just reply to this tweet with the idea (and if you think this approach is wrong, would love to hear that too).

Thanks!
Jeff

— Jeff Bezos (@JeffBezos) Jun. 15, 2017

As an example of the kind of near-term effort he has in mind, Mr. Bezos singled out a commitment Amazon recently made to provide a homeless shelter for families, Mary's Place, with a permanent home in a new Amazon office building that will be built starting later this year.

The prospect of someone with Mr. Bezos's wealth — he is the second-richest person in the world, according to the Bloomberg Billionaires Index, with a fortune of well over $80 billion — increasing his giving was greeted enthusiastically by people who work in philanthropy. His approach is unusual compared with many big philanthropists from the technology field, like Bill Gates, a founder of Microsoft, whose foundation has tackled long-term global health problems like malaria, among other challenges.

"I would call it surprising, but welcome," said Jacob Harold, the president of Guidestar, a national database of nonprofits. "It's rare for big-dollar donors to be honest about their desire for short-term results."

Mr. Harold said that he "would be worried if every donor was saying this," but that Mr. Bezos's approach could have a meaningful effect.

Mr. Bezos did not say on Twitter how much money he planned to commit to philanthropic giving. Given the magnitude of his wealth and the generosity of others in technology like Mr. Gates, his philanthropy has been relatively modest. He and his family have donated $15 million to Princeton University, his alma mater, and recently gave $35 million to the Fred Hutchinson Cancer Research Center in Seattle, the largest donation in that institution's history.

Mr. Bezos has also characterized Blue Origin, the for-profit space company that he is funding with about $1 billion of his wealth annually, as an effort to help save Earth in the long run by providing means to move heavy industry off the planet.

Mr. Bezos asked people to reply to his post with their ideas. A little more than five hours after his request, there were more than 3,600 such replies, including suggestions for contributing to affordable housing, veterans' organizations and lesbian, gay, bisexual and transgender causes.

Larry Brilliant, the acting chairman of the Skoll Global Threats Fund, a philanthropy created by Jeff Skoll, one of eBay's founders, said that crowdsourcing philanthropic ideas had had mixed success in large part because of the challenge of identifying ones that have promise.

"The denominator of ideas you will get in, the vast majority of ideas which are not good, not viable, will flood this process," said Mr. Brilliant, who formerly ran Google's philanthropic arm.

Move Over, Bill Gates. Jeff Bezos Gets a Turn as World's Richest Person.

BY NICK WINGFIELD | JULY 27, 2017

SEATTLE — Jeff Bezos on Thursday took something away from a billionaire neighbor in the Seattle area, Bill Gates — the mantle of world's richest person.

A 1 percent pop early in the day in the shares of Amazon.com — the internet company Mr. Bezos founded, which accounts for the vast majority of his wealth — was enough to bump him over the wealth of Mr. Gates, the philanthropist and Microsoft co-founder, according to a real-time list of billionaires by Forbes.com, which has tallied the fortunes of the uber-rich for decades.

Forbes estimated the wealth of Mr. Bezos, currently Amazon's chief executive, at $90.6 billion, compared with $90 billion for Mr. Gates. Later in the day, Amazon's shares cooled slightly, allowing Mr. Gates to regain the top position. The back and forth could continue depending on the fluctuations in Amazon shares.

Mr. Bezos has added tens of billions of dollars in wealth — at least on paper — over the last year as Amazon shares surged more than 40 percent during that time period. They traded at about $1,063 on Thursday, ahead of the release of the company's latest earnings report.

According to a filing with securities regulators in April, Mr. Bezos holds nearly 81 million shares of Amazon — almost 17 percent of the company. Forbes also estimates the value of his other investments — including his ownership of The Washington Post and the rocket company Blue Origin — and cash from the sale of securities as part of its wealth calculations. Mr. Bezos has said he sells about $1 billion a year worth of Amazon stock to finance Blue Origin.

Mr. Gates has been at the top of the Forbes list of billionaires for 18 of the last 23 years.

Jeff Bezos, the founder and chief executive of Amazon.

Most of Mr. Gates's wealth originates from Microsoft. The company's stock has risen to new highs lately. A Microsoft filing from October said he held nearly 191 million shares of Microsoft — about 2.46 percent of its stock — which are currently worth about $14.1 billion.

But Mr. Gates has spent years diversifying his investments.

Kerry Dolan, an assistant managing editor for Forbes, said the publication also considers extensive assets Mr. Gates holds through his Cascade Investments, which has stakes in private equity, real estate and public companies. Forbes does not include his more than $31 billion in contributions to the Bill & Melinda Gates Foundation in its wealth calculations.

Drew Herdener, a spokesman for Amazon, declined to comment on Mr. Bezos's move to the top of the Forbes list. Naomi Zeitlin, a spokeswoman for Mr. Gates, declined to comment.

Jeff Bezos, Mr. Amazon, Steps Out

BY NICK WINGFIELD AND NELLIE BOWLES | JAN. 12, 2018

Mr. Bezos is the world's richest person and can afford virtually any luxury. But obscurity is no longer among them.

SEATTLE — Jeff Bezos rubbed elbows last weekend with Halle Berry, Chris Hemsworth and other Hollywood celebrities at an after-party for the Golden Globes. In December, he walked the red carpet, along with Meryl Streep and Tom Hanks, at a screening of "The Post" in Washington.

On Friday, Mr. Bezos and his wife, MacKenzie, made public their $33 million donation to a nonprofit that provides college scholarships to so-called Dreamers, young immigrants brought to the United States illegally as children. In October, he received an award for a donation to a marriage equality campaign.

Jennifer Cast, an Amazon executive who solicited the donation from him, said at the event that they could have donated anonymously to the campaign. "But just as critical as the money was Jeff's offer to let us publicly acknowledge their gifts," she said.

"By allowing us to take their donation public," she added, "the world quickly knew that Jeff Bezos supported marriage equality."

The appearances and actions are a new look for Mr. Bezos.

As he was shaping Amazon into one of the world's most valuable companies, Mr. Bezos developed a reputation as a brilliant but mysterious and coldblooded corporate titan. He preferred to hunker down in Amazon's hometown, Seattle, at least partly because he thought it was better for Amazon's growing business, largely avoiding public causes and the black-tie circuit.

But while Mr. Bezos — who at 54 is the world's richest person, with a net worth of more than $100 billion — can afford virtually any luxury, obscurity is no longer among them.

Amazon, now a behemoth valued at more than $600 billion, has become one of the faces of "big tech," along with Apple, Alphabet's Google and Facebook. These companies are facing a backlash. Amazon is under the microscope for what critics say is its corrosive effect on jobs and competition, and Mr. Bezos has become a bête noire for President Trump, who repeatedly singles out him and Amazon for scorn on Twitter.

"People are starting to get scared of Amazon," said Steve Case, a co-founder of America Online, who recently started an investment fund focused on start-ups in underserved areas, with Mr. Bezos among its contributors. "If Jeff continues to hang out in Seattle, he's going to get a lot more incoming. Even for just defense reasons, he has to now play offense."

Mr. Bezos's portfolio of other ventures has thrust him farther into the spotlight. In October 2013, he bought The Washington Post for $250 million, jump-starting a renaissance of the paper. In 2016, Mr. Bezos bought a $23 million home in Washington, one of the city's most expensive, which is undergoing extensive renovations to make it a suitable party spot for the city's political class. Nearby neighbors include former President Barack Obama and his family, and Mr. Trump's daughter Ivanka Trump and her husband, Jared Kushner.

Mr. Bezos's space start-up, Blue Origin, is also making its efforts more public, giving him another stage. The company is trying to rescue Earth by helping to move pollution-belching heavy industries off the planet.

"He's getting thanked at the Golden Globes and targeted by presidential tweet tantrums — not even Steve Jobs had that kind of pop-culture currency," said Margaret O'Mara, a professor of history at the University of Washington, who curated a museum exhibit in Seattle endowed by Mr. Bezos.

In a statement, Drew Herdener, an Amazon spokesman, said, "Jeff loves what he is doing, at Amazon, Blue Origin and The Washington Post, and he enjoys sharing his enthusiasm in public as he works with the teams to build and invent."

Mr. Bezos outside a reusable space vehicle designed by Blue Origin, a start-up that has helped expand his public exposure.

But interviews with more than 30 people who know Mr. Bezos, most of whom declined to be identified to protect their relationships with him, revealed his awareness of the growing opposition to Amazon and his growing comfort with being in the public eye.

Mr. Bezos, they said, accepts the probability of greater government scrutiny of Amazon. The chief executive has advised Amazon executives to conduct themselves so that they can pass any legal or regulatory test.

The investor Warren E. Buffett, who has known Mr. Bezos since the 1990s, said the cautionary tale of Microsoft, which faced a landmark antitrust case by the government that decade, must loom in Mr. Bezos's mind. Microsoft, by far the most dominant technology company at the time, lost its footing after the case, opening an unexpected opportunity for competitors.

"You're going to get a lot of scrutiny if you're disrupting other people's livelihoods," Mr. Buffett said.

Some of the people who know Mr. Bezos said his new public face was for business expediency. Others believe it is a result of personal growth.

But they all said it was clear that Mr. Bezos and Amazon were trying to go beyond his tech persona to show the world his other sides.

HIDING IN PLAIN SIGHT

Mr. Bezos has always been happy to play the role of Amazon's chief pitchman, especially when he perceives some benefit to Amazon customers from doing so, people who have worked with him said. He submits to interviews and speaks at events when, for instance, a new company product like the Kindle electronic reader or Echo speaker needs to be explained to the world.

But for nearly two decades, he was adamant that the company should largely stay out of the political limelight and not make a stir in local communities. It also had a bare-bones lobbying operation.

Even as he was named Time magazine's person of the year in 1999, he tried to avoid politics. He was even reluctant to do photo opportunities with politicians, standard fare for executives, one longtime former employee said.

There were business benefits to staying out of the glare.

A hedge fund executive in New York who caught the internet bug early, Mr. Bezos piled into a vehicle with his wife in 1994 with the intention of finding a place to start a business selling books on the internet. He founded Amazon later that year in Seattle, in part because of the growing pool of technical talent Microsoft had brought to the area.

But putting his start-up in Washington also meant Amazon would not have to collect sales tax in the country's most populous states, like California, Texas and New York. Retailers typically have an obligation to collect sales tax in states where they have a physical presence.

For a time, for the same reason, the company would not publicly discuss where most of its warehouses were. And Amazon employees in Seattle who planned to travel out of state for work had to submit itineraries for review to avoid triggering unwanted sales tax liabilities.

An employee sorts bins at an Amazon warehouse in Florence, N.J. The company's agreements with states to pay sales taxes, allowing it to build facilities across the country, was a turning point for Mr. Bezos.

Those efforts would, in turn, give his fledgling company a further price advantage against established physical retailers like Barnes & Noble.

It also meant that, despite its growing legions of customers, Amazon remained almost invisible in politics.

By the end of 2012, the company had swelled to more than 88,000 employees and over $61 billion in annual sales, creating huge businesses like its Prime membership service and Amazon Web Services along the way. Yet that year the company was criticized by leaders in Seattle and the news media for being disengaged from civic life compared with stalwarts like Boeing and Starbucks.

"I'm not aware of what Amazon does in the community," Sally Jewell, the chief executive of the retailer R.E.I. at the time, said in The Seattle Times in 2012. "It's not a name that comes up often in the nonprofit organizations I'm involved with."

With investors, Mr. Bezos gave just enough of a peek at Amazon's business to win their confidence while saying as little as possible to keep competitors guessing. To this day, Amazon will not disclose exactly how many Kindles, Echoes and other devices it has sold, and for years it refused to reveal financial details about Amazon Web Services, its highly profitable cloud computing business.

Despite the paucity of details, investors have sent its stock up more than 1,100 percent over the last decade, dazzled by its growth.

A GROWING SPOTLIGHT

A turning point came for Mr. Bezos around 2011 when Amazon faced a public showdown with state governments.

At the time, legislators began hounding internet retailers like Amazon to collect sales tax. In California, Amazon initially campaigned to overturn a new law imposing an internet sales tax. But Mr. Bezos backed off after it became clear that Amazon's image could be tarnished, a former employee involved in the matter said.

Instead, Amazon began to make peace. In 2011, it signed an agreement with California to collect sales tax in the state, reaching numerous similar agreements around the same time.

As part of those state deals, Amazon began building warehouses across the country, which allowed Amazon to deliver orders more quickly and let local politicians trumpet the arrival of thousands of jobs.

Suddenly, a company that once refused to confirm how many employees it had at its Seattle headquarters could not stop talking about how many jobs it was creating. It now has 542,000 employees.

As Mr. Bezos and the company talked about creating jobs, though, he and Amazon faced a counternarrative from critics that the company was really a job-killing bully.

Waves of store closings by bricks-and-mortar retailers like Barnes & Noble and Macy's increased the volume. "Amazon Must Be Stopped," read a 2014 New Republic article about the company's growing market power.

That year, a nasty fight over e-book prices with Hachette, the book publisher, solidified Amazon's reputation for using brass-knuckle tactics. At one point, Amazon slowed delivery times for the publisher's titles and took other steps to make them less attractive to order.

After the matter was resolved, Mr. Bezos told an interviewer that Amazon was simply negotiating hard on behalf of its customers.

"It's very difficult for incumbents who have a sweet thing to accept change," he said, referring to book publishers.

Another blow to the company's public standing landed in 2015 when The New York Times published a lengthy examination of Amazon's corporate work culture, which was depicted as an unforgiving environment. "The article doesn't describe the Amazon I know or the caring Amazonians I work with every day," Mr. Bezos said in an email to the company's employees after the article came out.

According to two people who work closely with Mr. Bezos, the chief executive became more focused on corporate reputation issues after The Times article and the Hachette uproar.

By late 2015, a few months after Mr. Trump announced his campaign for president, he started his Twitter broadsides against Mr. Bezos, which often coincided with critical coverage of the candidate in The Washington Post.

"The @washingtonpost loses money (a deduction) and gives owner @JeffBezos power to screw public on low taxation of @Amazon!" he tweeted in December that year. "Big tax shelter."

Mr. Bezos responded by offering to launch the future president of the United States into space on a Blue Origin rocket.

A White House spokesman did not respond to requests for comment.

The attention in Washington edged up in June when Amazon announced it was buying Whole Foods Markets. Though Amazon remains a niche player in the grocery business, the deal drove home the power of the company and led some lawmakers to question its power.

"The purchase of Whole Foods was a moment when people looked up and recognized this company as a force in the economy," said Stacy Mitchell, a co-director of the Institute for Local Self-Reliance, a non-profit advocacy group for local businesses, which has published a critical report on Amazon's impact on jobs and communities.

MR. BEZOS GOES TO THE OTHER WASHINGTON

People who have known Mr. Bezos for a long time say they see a concerted effort by him and Amazon to show more of his personality.

He became an active user of Twitter in late 2015, posting a photo of himself wearing his lucky cowboy boots and a video clip of him standing atop a wind turbine in Texas. At an event with his brother in Los Angeles in November, as part of a long lineup of presentations by an array of business, wellness and entertainment leaders, he said his ideal job would be bartender, partly because he enjoys talking to people.

"I pride myself on my craft cocktails," he said.

If there's an image that captures Mr. Bezos at the moment, it's a picture of him with his biceps bulging out of a polo shirt at a business conference in Idaho from July. "Swole Jeff Bezos" instantly became an internet meme, with one tweet juxtaposing shots of a doughy Mr. Bezos from the late 1990s (caption: "I sell books") and the brawny 2017 version ("I sell whatever I want").

The details people are willing to talk about include scraps about his daily routine. On most days, he leaves his lakefront estate in the affluent town of Medina, Wash., for a sparkling new 37-story office tower in Seattle, where he runs Amazon.

On Wednesdays, he heads south to an industrial office park in the suburb of Kent, where rockets are assembled for Blue Origin.

Every other week, he huddles on conference calls with The Post's leadership, and twice a year they visit him at his home. He communicates with the newspaper's top brass with an email list called the Pancakes Group. The Amazon chief once made members of the group flapjacks from a favorite recipe in "Joy of Cooking" on their first visit to his house.

Mr. Bezos's ownership has jump-started a renaissance at The Washington Post.

"It wasn't like we went to some billionaire's house and the help outnumbered the guests," said Shailesh Prakash, the newspaper's chief information officer. "He was trying to get the dog off the couch."

Mr. Bezos's more public-facing work was abetted by a management change nearly two years ago at Amazon, when he put Jeff Wilke in charge of its consumer business and Andy Jassy in charge of cloud computing. That freed him up to devote more time to The Post and Blue Origin, though he remains deeply engaged at Amazon, dedicating most of his time to initiatives that are two to four years away from hitting the market.

Mr. Bezos has also pushed using publicity to the company's advantage. In September, he masterminded the company's splashy search for a place to locate a second headquarters. In the hoopla, Amazon highlighted the jobs it planned to create with the move — up to 50,000 total — and spurred a horde of towns, from Dallas to Boston, to apply.

In the future, that means Mr. Bezos will most likely be a more familiar presence in Washington. Mr. Bezos now visits Washington about 10 times a year, dropping in at The Post for forums, discussions with engineers and meals with journalists. In the capital's stately Kalorama neighborhood, just off Massachusetts Avenue's row of embassies, renovations are proceeding on his home — two combined properties that used to be the city's Textile Museum.

Mr. Bezos plans to host salon-style dinners at the house, drawing inspiration from the celebrated dinner parties thrown by Katharine Graham, the former publisher of The Post, for the city's movers and shakers from both parties. Mr. Bezos is known for asking his dinner guests to stick to a single conversation topic at a time to keep people from splintering off into private side discussions.

"It's a very big house," said Martin Baron, the executive editor of The Post. "I hope he has a party for us in the house."

Sally Quinn, a longtime Post writer and an arbiter of the city's social mores, said she had no firsthand knowledge of Mr. Bezos's plans for his home. But she praised the idea of attempting to bring together guests from across the political spectrum.

"There's really no one who is doing that kind of thing in Washington right now," said Ms. Quinn, who bumped into Mr. Bezos recently at the screening of "The Post." "It would be like a throwback to the old days."

"I think Jeff," she said, "is the only person who could do that."

NICK WINGFIELD reported from Seattle, and NELLIE BOWLES from San Francisco. BROOKS BARNES contributed reporting from Los Angeles, and CECILIA KANG from Washington. DORIS BURKE contributed research.

Amazon Hits $1,000,000,000,000 in Value, Following Apple

BY DAVID STREITFELD | SEPT. 4, 2018

SAN FRANCISCO — When Apple's market value crossed a trillion dollars last month, the reason was simple: It makes devices that a lot of people are willing to spend a lot of money on.

Now Amazon has become the second American company to cross that once-unimaginable line. Its shares rose as high as $2,050.50 on Tuesday morning, pushing it over $1 trillion in value, before immediately falling back and then ending the day at $2,039.51, below the $1 trillion threshold. Amazon's founder and chief executive, Jeff Bezos, is worth nearly as much as Bill Gates and Warren E. Buffett put together.

This time, the explanation is more complicated.

Amazon captures 49 cents of every e-commerce dollar in the United States. It employs more than 550,000 people and generates $178 billion in annual revenue. It sells everything from computing space to peanut butter to appointments with plumbers.

But the thing it has always sold the most — to investors, customers, the news media — is excitement.

In the beginning, Amazon was an exciting new way to shop for books: online. Then it was an exciting new way to read (Kindle e-books), an exciting new way to publish (CreateSpace), an exciting new way to power the internet (Amazon Web Services), an exciting new way to get deliveries (Amazon Prime), an exciting new way to make your house a high-tech outpost (Alexa).

Long before Amazon went to Hollywood and began making movies, it was the star of its own show, generating vast amounts of attention just for being Amazon. No other company had ever managed to turn its lack of profit into such effective drama, or the question of what its next move would be.

Amazon's search for a second headquarters — the company having run out of room and patience in its hometown, Seattle — set off a nationwide frenzy among politicians. Mr. Bezos even gamified his philanthropic plans, taking to Twitter to solicit advice about what he should do. (One popular recommendation: Pay your warehouse workers more.) Would Amazon collapse, or would it eat the world? It was the corporation-as-reality series, and it has been a long-running hit.

Public companies usually live under the tyranny of Wall Street, which prizes profits to the exclusion of all else. When Facebook and Twitter recently purged their rolls of fake users and began devoting more effort to cleaning up their acts, Wall Street did not applaud this civic-minded move but pummeled their shares.

Mr. Bezos made clear when Amazon went public in 1997 that he would not work for Wall Street, and the result was a company cast in an entirely different mold. It never feared losing money. In a real sense, there were no consequences for being wrong.

Behind the drama is a relentless and sometimes scary ambition. Amazon is the Jay Gatsby of American companies, believing that tomorrow it will run faster, stretch its arms out farther, fulfill the desires of consumers in ways that no other business possibly could. You will live in Amazon's world, it says, and you will like it.

The retailer has retained this futuristic luster even as Facebook, Twitter and Google, which promoted their own versions of technoparadise, have become suspect. It has retained its allure even as many of its ventures have tanked. Remember Kindle Singles? They were electronic articles hailed as the virtual reinvention of nonfiction. No one even noticed when the program fizzled.

"We like to go down unexplored alleys and see what's at the end. Sometimes they're dead ends," Mr. Bezos said in 2009. "Sometimes they open up into broad avenues and we find something really exciting."

One of the great benefits for Amazon of this approach is that it is impossible to tell where reality ends and hype — or perhaps even madness — begins.

Take Amazon's drone program, which it first announced on "60 Minutes." "I know this looks like science fiction," Mr. Bezos said, as he showed a film of an unmanned vehicle delivering a package. "It's not." He said there were "years of additional work" to be done, but declared himself an optimist. Drone delivery, he predicted, would be a reality in "four, five years."

That was December 2013. Roughly a million features were written about Amazon and its drones, nearly all with the subtext: Isn't this the coolest thing ever?

Over the years, the company kept raising the stakes, as if they were not already high enough. Amazon applied a few years ago for a patent for an "aerial fulfillment center" that would float at 45,000 feet. Drones would fly out of it with your order and then glide down to your backyard.

What delivery could possibly be important enough to merit such a crazy system? The patent has a suggestion: "Prepared hot food." We wanted flying cars, but we got flying burritos instead.

The fulfillment center, which looks in drawings like a blimp tugging a warehouse, has other uses besides delivering dinner. It would drift down to 2,000 feet to what the patent calls "the advertising altitude," where it would present information "about items and/or services." Perhaps it will be just like the movie "Blade Runner," and the floating ads will trumpet the joys of working in Amazon's off-world colonies. The patent was granted this summer.

Still not impressed? This year, Amazon got a patent to more or less bomb people with their packages. The drone would drop the burrito or Stephen King blockbuster from a height of as much as 25 feet, in theory cushioning the plunge with an airbag.

Haye Kesteloo, senior editor of the news site DroneDJ, noted that there were many hurdles to routine delivery by drone, even if the vehicles are not being launched from airships. The claimed drone attack on President Nicolás Maduro in Venezuela will not help soothe nervous citizens.

Nevertheless, Mr. Kesteloo, like Mr. Bezos, proclaims himself an optimist. "Companies like Amazon will make routine drone deliveries to consumers by 2025," he said — only twice as far away as promised.

There are reasons to be skeptical about even this schedule. But that's the magic of Amazon. Even if the drones do not pan out, they have kept attention focused on the company, fulfilling a different part of the business plan. There is scarcely any oxygen left to discuss the more contentious aspects of Amazon, like its scorn for taxes or its plans to capture much of local government purchasing.

"There is no doubt anymore," said Ron Nussbaum, who runs an investment management fund called Maverick Value in Los Angeles. "The stock always goes up, and no one doubts it will keep going up."

Mr. Nussbaum, who emphasized that over all his investments were profitable, might be the last Amazon skeptic. "It's an honor," he said.

And an expensive one. Last year, when Amazon crossed $1,000 a share, he started buying "put" options — bets that the stock would decline. One of his puts has dropped 85 percent; another, 92 percent.

Mr. Nussbaum is planning to buy more. He thinks people are confusing their impressions of Amazon the company with Amazon as an investment.

"If I fill up your gas tank for $1 but it costs me $2, you can say it's a great product, but it doesn't make any sense as a company," he said.

Apple had profits of $48 billion last year. Amazon's were less than a tenth of that. If profits were all that mattered, Amazon should be worth about $100 billion, the size of United Technologies or Texas Instruments. That is nothing to sneeze at, but nothing to get people excited, either.

Even before Amazon hit $1 trillion, the milestone was old news. There was a poll on Facebook run by a group of young Wall Street investors. The question: Would Amazon or Apple be the first to hit $2 trillion?

The vote was overwhelmingly in favor of Amazon. Dreams will always triumph over devices.

Why Jeff Bezos Should Push for Nobody to Get as Rich as Jeff Bezos

COLUMN | BY FARHAD MANJOO | SEPT. 19, 2018

JEFF BEZOS, the founder of Amazon and the world's wealthiest man, has been publicly agonizing over a vexing problem: what to do with all his money.

Last week, more than a year after asking his Twitter followers for philanthropic ideas, Mr. Bezos and his wife, MacKenzie, announced an initial plan. They said they would donate $2 billion to a new foundation meant to address homelessness and improve preschool education. The gift is a tiny portion of the Bezoses' total wealth — estimated by Forbes magazine to be $162 billion — but the foundation's name, the Bezos Day 1 Fund, suggests there will be lots more to come.

The question of how Mr. Bezos should spend his money is a good one, but a better place to start might be: Why does he have so much money in the first place? What does his fortune tell us about the economic structure and impact of the tech industry, the engine behind his billions? And, most important, what responsibility comes with his wealth — and is it any business of ours what he does with it?

The answer: Of course it's our business.

Mr. Bezos's extreme wealth is not only a product of his own ingenuity. It is also a function of several grand forces shaping the global economy. One is the unequal impact of digital technology, which has reduced costs and brought conveniences to many, but whose direct economic benefits have accrued to a small number of superstar companies and their largest shareholders. There is also the effect of labor and economic policy, which in the United States has failed to keep up with, and often only aggravated, the problem of tech-driven concentrations of wealth.

Once you understand the forces pushing Mr. Bezos's fortune ever skyward, one strategy for how he might spend it emerges above all others. "I think the most important thing he can do with his money is

DOUG CHAYKA

to become a traitor to his class," said Anand Giridharadas, author of a new book, "Winners Take All."

In the book, Mr. Giridharadas argues that the efforts of the super-wealthy to change the world through philanthropy are often a distraction from the planet's actual problems. To truly fix the world, Mr. Bezos ought to push for policy changes that would create a more equal distribution of the winnings derived from a tech-driven economy, Mr. Giridharadas said.

"He should address himself to America's deepest problems in ways that would demand sacrifice from the winners of our age — making a difference at the expense of their opportunity to make a killing," Mr. Giridharadas said.

There's another way of putting this: Jeff Bezos should spend his vast fortune pushing for a society where no one can ever become as rich as Jeff Bezos is now.

An Amazon spokesman declined to comment on Mr. Bezos's philanthropic plans.

Those who are fans of Amazon may argue with the notion that Mr. Bezos's wealth represents a problem and a responsibility. After all, Bezos, 54, is an uncommonly gifted businessman. He acquired his wealth legally and in the most quintessentially American way: He had a wacky idea, took a stab at it, stuck with it through thick and thin, and, through patient, deliberate, farsighted risk-taking, created one of the most innovative companies of the modern era.

But Mr. Bezos isn't just rich. He is growing unprecedentedly rich — rich enough that his wealth, by itself, illustrates a new economic reality.

A year ago, when he first called for philanthropy ideas, Mr. Bezos's fortune was estimated at only $80 billion, putting him an embarrassing second on the rich-person list, behind Bill Gates. The ideas rolled in, but the money came in faster. As Amazon's stock price sailed ever higher, Mr. Bezos's fortune eclipsed Mr. Gates's — and then kept climbing.

"The only way that I can see to deploy this much financial resource is by converting my Amazon winnings into space travel," Mr. Bezos told an interviewer in April.

In July, Mr. Bezos's wealth surpassed $150 billion, a record; even if inflation is accounted for, he is almost certainly the wealthiest human being in modern history. Only John D. Rockefeller, whose fortune once exceeded 2 percent of the total American economy, might plausibly have been richer. (Mr. Bezos would need to double his wealth again to beat that standard.)

Most of Mr. Bezos's wealth is tied up in Amazon's stock, so he could well lose billions if Amazon flails. But if he does, there will probably be someone else just as megarich to take his place, because extreme concentrations of wealth are baked into the dynamics of the modern tech economy.

Tech-powered businesses are often driven by an economic concept known as network effects, in which the very popularity of a service sparks even greater popularity. Amazon, for instance, keeps attracting more third-party businesses to sell goods in its store — which in turn makes it a better store for customers, which attracts more suppliers, improving the customer experience, and so on in an endless virtuous cycle. Digital businesses are also characterized by tremendous economies of scale — Amazon can create a robotic assistant once and deploy it to everyone — that further entrench concentration.

"We have technology that has allowed us to create vastly more wealth for society," said Erik Brynjolfsson, director of the M.I.T. Initiative on the Digital Economy. "But there's no economic law that says that these benefits will be distributed evenly — and it's worked out that some people have gotten most of the benefits and a lot of other people have been left behind."

But economics isn't destiny, he said.

"Technology has led to some of this concentration, but since it makes the pie bigger, you could make everyone better off simultaneously — you could make the poor better off and the rich better off — and whether we do that is a matter of policy," he said.

As Annie Lowrey pointed out in The Atlantic last month, economic policy is currently tilted toward benefiting people like Mr. Bezos far more than the hundreds of thousands of people who work in his warehouses. Among other policies, Amazon has capitalized on a weakened union movement and a low minimum wage, which has allowed it to expand by hiring an army of workers for its warehouses.

Amazon said that on average, its full-time warehouse workers made $15 an hour, including wages and other compensation; the company also said it provided full benefits, including tuition for career skills, to those workers. A $15 wage is higher than at some other retailers, but it is lower than estimates for what a family in the United States needs to meet its basic needs, known as a living wage.

"They're not providing the sort of high-wage, middle-class jobs to a broad swath of individuals that we used to associate with corporate success," Lawrence Katz, an economist at Harvard, said of Amazon and other high-flying tech firms. "What we're seeing is not the sharing of the productivity benefits that we used to see in the past. And that may be even more galling than the concentration of wealth."

How could Mr. Bezos address these issues through philanthropy? Mr. Giridharadas suggested several liberal economic policy ideas, among them efforts to strengthen unions, equalize how we pay for education, increase minimum-wage laws and push for a more progressive tax system. Both Mr. Gates and Warren Buffett — the second- and third-wealthiest people in the world — have said they should pay higher taxes.

Those ideas strike me as unlikely; Mr. Bezos is a far-thinking innovator, but he has expressed little interest in near-term political questions.

On the other hand, Mr. Bezos's most attractive quality, as a businessman, is his capacity for patience and surprise.

"This is guy who was willing to buck what everyone else thought for so long," Mr. Giridharadas said. "If he brings that same irreverence to the question of how to give, he has the potential to interrogate himself about why it is that we need so many billionaires to save us in the first place — and what we could do to build a society that would not require Jeff Bezos to help us so much."

"State of the Art" is a column from Farhad Manjoo that examines how technology is changing business and society.

How Jeff Bezos Went to Hollywood and Lost Control

BY AMY CHOZICK | MARCH 2, 2019

JEFF BEZOS AMASSED the world's greatest fortune by relying on what he has called a "regret minimization framework." He built an $800 billion company with 14 codified principles and a brutally exacting culture. His annual salary of $81,840 has not budged since 1998.

But then Mr. Bezos went to Hollywood.

In the weeks since the Amazon founder tweeted that he and his wife of 25 years were divorcing, he has gone to war with a grocery store tabloid and escalated a conflict with the president of the United States. And he has essentially ceded control of his own narrative to two rogue characters: a swashbuckling A-list security consultant, Gavin de Becker, and his girlfriend's fame-hungry brother-manager, Michael Sanchez. Locked in a feud, the two are prolonging the scandal's news value almost daily.

Mr. Bezos is at the center of an honest-to-God melodrama, full of salacious revelations, family betrayals and international intrigue. In Seattle, Amazon's senior vice president for global corporate affairs, the former White House press secretary Jay Carney, has recently tried to get the story back under control. But in Hollywood, the swirl around Mr. Bezos's love life refuses to be contained, churning through an ecosystem of gossip and favors, where dish on the rich and powerful is currency.

Amazon executives were blindsided by a sequence of events that began in early January: the announcement by Jeff and MacKenzie Bezos of their divorce; the 11-page National Enquirer exposé that Mr. Bezos was romantically involved with Lauren Sanchez, a former Los Angeles TV anchor; a sensational blog post by Mr. Bezos accusing the head of the tabloid, an ally of President Trump, of attempting to extort him over a "below-the-belt selfie" and other sexts.

ELIZABETH LIPPMAN FOR THE NEW YORK TIMES

The Amazon billionaire Jeff Bezos after the Golden Globes in January. In Hollywood, the swirl around his love life refuses to be contained.

It has not helped matters that the intimate details of Mr. Bezos's personal life emerged around the same time that the company abruptly canceled its plans to build a new headquarters in New York, after fighting with lawmakers and activists. People who have worked closely with Mr. Bezos have watched dumbfounded that a man famous for being a vault of discretion could end up, as one of them put it, in the middle of such a "clown show."

For advice on the crisis, Mr. Bezos has relied almost entirely on Mr. de Becker, who in addition to providing security to stars is something of a celebrity himself. He once protected Cher, and he delivered a eulogy at the memorial of his friend Carrie Fisher. His book, "The Gift of Fear," was a megahit — Oprah Winfrey backed it — and reads like a TED Talk for the rich and afraid.

Mr. de Becker is employed by Mr. Bezos, not Amazon, and appears to be hardly in touch with strategists at the company. Adding to the cast, Mr. de Becker has enlisted the famed law firm Boies Schiller Flexner, as well as Marty Singer, a notorious Los Angeles litigator who has represented John Travolta and Sharon Stone, to work the media.

Ms. Sanchez has consulted the Los Angeles divorce maestro Laura Wasser, who has counted Kim Kardashian West and Angelina Jolie as clients. Also in the mix is Ms. Sanchez's estranged husband, Patrick Whitesell, who as the executive chairman of Endeavor is one of the most powerful figures in Hollywood. His business partner at the agency is the operatically colorful macher Ari Emanuel, and they know more than almost anyone about how to use tabloid ink to boost a client or break a competitor.

After the affair broke into the open, it didn't take long for Mr. Whitesell to be spotted by TMZ leaving a nightclub with a 20-something model. Her surname? Alexa.

AN EXPANDING CAST OF ONLY-IN-L.A. CHARACTERS

The loosest cannon of them all may be Michael Sanchez. Ms. Sanchez's brother is a scrappy agent to a roster of reality TV personalities and an incorrigible gossip even in a town full of them. He is also a supporter of Mr. Trump, and has relationships with some of his operatives, including Roger Stone and Carter Page. Mr. Sanchez is in regular touch with an expanding list of reporters around the country, and is constantly supplying them with fresh innuendo on the Bezos drama.

Mr. Sanchez alleges that Mr. de Becker is trying to keep his sister away from Mr. Bezos, in hopes of keeping the Bezos marriage intact. "Gavin has brilliantly set you and I up with the clear goal of destroying your love for my sister," Mr. Sanchez wrote in an email to Mr. Bezos on Valentine's Day, a copy of which was reviewed by The New York Times. "I know the truth about your love for Lauren and her love for you."

Four people with direct knowledge of the siblings' relationship said that Ms. Sanchez is no longer speaking to her brother. Mr. Sanchez disputed this, and Ms. Sanchez declined to comment.

In February, The Daily Beast reported that Mr. de Becker had completed an investigation into who initially leaked the texts, and that Mr. Sanchez provided The Enquirer with its exclusive on Mr. Bezos's affair. In an interview, Mr. Sanchez told me he did talk to the tabloid about his sister's relationship (in an effort to help her), but denied sending it Mr. Bezos's sexts, which he said he didn't have access to. He theorized that The Enquirer had obtained the images via a Beverly Hills socialite who had gotten them directly from his sister.

I explained to two people with direct knowledge of The Enquirer's reporting what Mr. Sanchez told me: that he'd provided some details of the affair to the tabloid, but not the sexts. These people, who would talk only about private conversations without attribution, emphasized that everything The Enquirer received on the Bezos affair, including the "below-the-belt selfie," came from a single source.

These people added that the source was compensated by The Enquirer. How much? An amount well above the $150,000 that the tabloid paid the former Playboy model Karen McDougal to keep quiet about her alleged affair with Mr. Trump ahead of the 2016 election, they said.

MR. BEZOS CHANGES HOLLYWOOD — AND VICE VERSA

For years, Mr. Bezos did not seem like the kind of chief executive who craved rock-star status. He didn't employ a personal publicist to help bolster the Bezos myth, because he didn't need to. The sheer reach of his company did the mythmaking for him: Amazon has transformed the way we read, shop and watch TV, and through its cloud services division runs an astonishingly large portion of the internet. Even as the company's power grew, Mr. Bezos made a point of directing focus to the customer, who he said occupied "the empty chair" in every meeting.

Mr. Bezos bought a home in Beverly Hills in 2007, as Amazon was beginning to expand into entertainment. The company does not break out the financials of its Hollywood business, but it has been spending furiously to build a TV and film portfolio that enriches its Prime offering. Subscription services brought in more than $14 billion last year. To Hollywood insiders, the gusher of cash turned Mr. Bezos into the object of fascination and fear.

As Amazon bulldozed its way into the industry, Mr. Bezos transformed from a low-key, geeky Seattle dad to a chiseled presence on the red carpet. He has never seemed to be enthralled with the filmmaking process — he leaves day-to-day management to the Amazon Studios chief Jennifer Salke — but like Howard Hughes and other outsider tycoons before him, Mr. Bezos has unmistakably embraced the industry's trappings.

His true Hollywood coming out was in 2016, when he gave a party — lavish even in the context of awards season — to celebrate the Oscar favorite "Manchester by the Sea," an Amazon Studios production. Matt Damon was the co-host. It was held in a temporary edifice (only in Beverly Hills could it be called a "tent") perched at the end of the long, pebbled driveway at Mr. Bezos's mansion, high above Sunset Boulevard. The evening appears to be the first time that he and Ms. Sanchez were publicly photographed together.

They had met the previous year. As Amazon pushed into entertainment, it often worked with Endeavor, and Mr. Whitesell and Ms. Sanchez started socializing with the Bezoses. Their children played together at the Bezos family's 29,000-square-foot compound outside Seattle, sprinting around a room decorated with NASA memorabilia and a chair in which J.K. Rowling wrote parts of the "Harry Potter" books. (It sold at auction for $394,000.)

Ms. Sanchez, an aviation enthusiast with a helicopter license, talked shop with Mr. Bezos, who spends much of his time building Blue Origin, his space exploration company. The two went flying together — encouraged by Mr. Whitesell, who saw the socializing as good for his wife's aerial film and production company, Black Ops Aviation.

By last year, they were having an affair. Three people in Ms. Sanchez's extended social circle said she was giddy and in love, showing amorous texts to a number of Brentwood and Beverly Hills moms.

At Amazon, Mr. Bezos has long implemented an idiosyncratic meeting structure. Executives sit in silence, reading a six-page memo on the topic at hand. Bullet points are frowned upon; the document must be a cogent narrative. Only once everyone has digested the "six-pager" do discussions begin.

That process may have been what Mr. Bezos was channeling when — without consulting Amazon brass — he published an explosive Medium essay on Feb. 7 accusing The Enquirer of extortion and blackmail. The tabloid was threatening to publish photos it had obtained, including one of Mr. Bezos's "semi-erect manhood," unless he met their conditions.

Mr. Bezos called out David Pecker, the chief executive of The Enquirer's parent company, American Media, who has been known to wield his influence to benefit Mr. Trump. (Last year, federal prosecutors determined that American Media had made illegal payments to silence women who said they had had affairs with Mr. Trump.)

Mr. Bezos added that he had asked Mr. de Becker to conduct an investigation into how the tabloid had gotten his texts and photos. He implied that Mr. Trump and the Saudi royal family's displeasure with The Washington Post, which he owns, were behind The Enquirer's actions.

When Mr. Bezos published his essay, commentators were nearly unanimous in hailing it as a public relations masterstroke: Somehow, the world's richest man, caught cheating on his wife, was now a victim.

But since then, more than three weeks have elapsed, and while Mr. de Becker has told The Washington Post that the Enquirer piece was "politically motivated," direct proof of the Trump or Saudi links has not yet emerged. Asked repeatedly for such evidence, Mr. de Becker, who was traveling in Fiji, declined to comment on the record.

A person in Mr. Bezos's camp, who was not authorized to speak on the record, said the investigation into the Enquirer story had moved beyond Mr. Sanchez, and to some extent was out of Mr. de Becker's hands, now that evidence was with law enforcement.

Mr. Bezos and Ms. Sanchez remain together. On Feb. 19, Mr. Bezos spoke at the Yale Club in New York about his plan to populate the solar system with one trillion people through Blue Origin. "I try to organize my personal time so that I live mostly about two to three years out," Mr. Bezos said, according to a transcript published on Business Insider. The New York Post elected to ignore the space-travel angle, reporting instead that he and Ms. Sanchez had been holed up in a Park Avenue "luxe love nest."

So far, investors haven't minded the messiness of Mr. Bezos's personal life and his pull toward Hollywood. Amazon's share price is up since the start of the year, and the company said that Mr. Bezos had not been distracted by the scandal. "Jeff remains as intensely focused on Amazon's various businesses as ever, running daylong meetings of the S-Team (our leadership team) and daily forwarding emails he receives from customers to business leaders," Mr. Carney wrote in an email.

Still, the incidents have left many adherents to the Bezos Way — who are legion — confused about what the events of the past several weeks say about Mr. Bezos's judgment.

One former Amazon executive, who signed a nondisclosure agreement and could only discuss the company anonymously, wondered how Mr. Bezos's behavior squared with a recent letter he sent to shareholders, in which he talked about irrevocable decisions, or what he called "one-way doors."

"These decisions must be made methodically, carefully, slowly and with great deliberation and consultation," Mr. Bezos said. "If you walk through and don't like what you see on the other side, you can't get back to where you were before."

BROOKS BARNES and **KAREN WEISE** contributed reporting.

Jeff Bezos, Amazon C.E.O., and MacKenzie Bezos Finalize Divorce Details

BY KAREN WEISE | APRIL 4, 2019

JEFF BEZOS, Amazon's founder and chief executive, and his wife, MacKenzie Bezos, said on Twitter on Thursday that they had finalized the details of their divorce.

Mr. Bezos will keep 75 percent of the couple's Amazon stock and all of their ownership of The Washington Post and the Blue Origin space company, Ms. Bezos wrote. Mr. Bezos will also have "sole voting authority" over Ms. Bezos's Amazon shares, according to a filing with the Securities and Exchange Commission.

After the divorce, Ms. Bezos will own roughly 4 percent of Amazon, a stake that was worth almost $36 billion on Thursday. By keeping 75 percent of the couple's Amazon shares, or about 12 percent of the company, Mr. Bezos will most likely remain the richest person in the world. His remaining stake in the company was worth almost $108 billion on Thursday. (Bill Gates, the second wealthiest, is worth $102 billion, according to Bloomberg.)

Experts had said that in Washington State, where Amazon is based and where the couple have been raising their four children, Ms. Bezos was entitled to roughly half of their assets. They have other investments and properties across the United States. The details of divorce settlements are not public, and theirs could contain other compensation for Ms. Bezos.

Ms. Bezos wrote on Twitter on Thursday that she was "excited about my own plans," without providing details. She has historically kept a low profile, focusing on her work as a novelist and on raising the couple's children.

Amazon declined to comment.

Their divorce filing caps four months of the kind of public drama that Amazon and its founder have long eschewed.

The couple announced their plan to split on Twitter in early January, saying that "after a long period of loving exploration and a trial separation, we have decided to divorce and continue our shared lives as friends." The news came as a surprise. Just a few months earlier they were spotted in a Miami nightclub celebrating their 25th anniversary.

After the news initially sent Amazon shares down, investors brushed it away, and the price rebounded.

But the relatively quiet disclosure took on new life a day later when The National Enquirer reported that Mr. Bezos was romantically involved with Lauren Sanchez, a former Los Angeles TV anchor. The tabloid published photos of the two together as well as intimate text messages.

Since then, Mr. Bezos and American Media Inc., the parent company of The National Enquirer, have been embroiled in a public feud.

Mr. Bezos published emails from American Media that he said amounted to "extortion and blackmail." He said the company had threatened to publish more embarrassing details, including a "below the belt selfie" that he had sent Ms. Sanchez. He insinuated that the leaks could have been politically motivated to harm him because of his ownership of The Washington Post. American Media denied those accusations.

On Saturday, Mr. Bezos's security consultant wrote an opinion article for The Daily Beast that said his team had "concluded with high confidence that the Saudis had access to Bezos's phone, and gained private information." He said the Saudis had targeted Mr. Bezos because of the newspaper's reporting on the murder of Jamal Khashoggi, one of its columnists, who United States officials believe was killed on the orders of the Saudi crown prince.

Mr. Bezos's consultant did not provide direct evidence of the accusation, nor did he say whether the Saudis had provided information to The Enquirer.

American Media flatly denied any Saudi involvement. It said that Ms. Sanchez's brother, Michael Sanchez, was the "sole source" of its investigation, and that "there was no involvement by any other third party whatsoever."

A Saudi official also said Saudi Arabia "categorically rejects all allegations" of being involved in the matter.

Despite all the drama, the Bezos divorce moved quickly, did not resort to court and was announced in unison.

"This is an example of how you would want to handle this kind of situation if you were a public figure," said Jennifer Payseno, a divorce lawyer who works with wealthy families in the Seattle area, where the Bezoses live.

"They are intertwined financially, so anything that helps him succeed helps her and vice versa," Ms. Payseno said.

After filing for divorce on Thursday, under state law the Bezoses must wait 90 days to submit their divorce decree to a court for approval.

Oprah at a Crossroads

BY CHRISTINE HAUGHNEY | NOV. 25, 2012

LOS ANGELES — It's not easy to find a fresh way to photograph Oprah Winfrey. That's why the editors of O, The Oprah Magazine, recently tried to create a shot that recalled the glory days of Ms. Winfrey's syndicated talk show. They arranged to photograph her for its April 2013 issue as she stepped onstage to speak to 5,000 attendees at the magazine's annual conference, a New Age slumber party of sorts for women held at the convention center here last month. When Ms. Winfrey confidently strode out dressed in a sea foam green V-neck dress and a pair of perilously tall ruby red stilettos, the audience collectively leapt to its feet and shrieked at the sight of her.

"I love you, Oprah," some women shouted, while other fans brushed away tears. "I love you back," she responded in her signature commanding voice. "It's no small thing to get the dough to come here."

Ms. Winfrey, who used to receive this kind of applause from fans five days a week, has had fewer such receptions since the talk show she hosted for 25 years ended 18 months ago. The cable network OWN, which she started with Discovery Communications, is emerging from low ratings and management shake-ups. And without a regular presence on daytime network television, she cannot steer traffic to her other products as easily as in the past. Her magazine, in particular, has experienced a decline in advertising revenue and newsstand sales since the talk show finished.

"She's still Oprah. But she's still struggling," said Janice Peck, an associate professor of journalism and mass communication at the University of Colorado who wrote the 2008 book "The Age of Oprah." "I think she's scared, even though she's very, very rich and she's always going to be very, very rich. The possibility of failure, it's quite scary."

Ms. Winfrey, 58, has shown some signs of strain. She arrived at the conference with faint shadows under her eyes and announced to her best friend, Gayle King, and the audience simultaneously that she had a breast cancer scare the week before. (It was ultimately a false alarm.) When Ms. King grew visibly upset, one woman chided Ms. Winfrey for not telling her friend ahead of time and ordered her to apologize to Ms. King — all before an audience. Ms. Winfrey also did not hide her dissatisfaction with the criticism she had faced. She told the audience, "the press tried to cut me off at the knees" in its coverage of OWN, and bristled at questions about the challenges her magazine confronted.

"I don't care what the form is," Ms. Winfrey said with the conviction of a preacher. "I care about what the message is."

With signs of progress at OWN, Ms. Winfrey now has more time to devote to other media platforms — her magazine, her radio channel on XM Satellite Radio, her Facebook page, which has 7.8 million subscribers, her Twitter account, which has nearly 15 million followers, and her latest content channel on The Huffington Post.

"It's all an opportunity to speak to people," Ms. Winfrey said as she sat for an interview during the conference, a pair of glittery gold stilettos slung in her hand and a couple of handlers in the corner quietly tapping away at smartphones. She pushed aside a bottle of sparkling water, a glass with a silver straw and a delicate orchid placed before her and spoke frankly about her plans.

"Ultimately, you have to make money because you are a business. I let other people worry about that. I worry about the message. I am always, always, always about holding true to the vision and the message, and when you are true to that, then people respond."

When it comes to the magazine, Ms. Winfrey said her staff prepared her to expect a 25 percent decline in newsstand sales after the talk show ended. (It has been closer to 22 percent.) And while she acknowledged that she enjoyed "holding the magazine in my hand," she was pragmatic about print's future and said she would stop publishing a print magazine if it were not profitable.

"Obviously, the show was helping in ways that you know I hadn't accounted for," Ms. Winfrey said. "I'm not interested, you know, in bleeding money."

Ms. Winfrey, who spoke in a conference room over the roars of an expectant crowd in the convention space below, said she knew that her brand's strength stemmed from how she resonated with a breadth of viewers.

"A little instinct that I had when I started the Oprah show in Chicago, I always knew it and it wasn't cockiness. It was just a knowingness that people are the same in Chicago as they are in Alabama as they are in Rhode Island as they are in Seattle," Ms. Winfrey said. "I knew that. I could feel that because I'm with the audience every day."

Ms. Winfrey wants that audience for the magazine, but she wants its readers to be younger. The median age for an O reader is 49, according to data tracked by the audience measurement company GfK MRI. (By comparison, Vogue's median is 35.6 and Real Simple's is 46.3.) Ms. Winfrey said she would like to attract women "in their 30s or perhaps their 20s, to be able to reach people when they are looking to fulfill their destiny." She added, "By the time you're 40, 42, you should have kind of figured it out already."

That may be a tougher climb. While articles in women's magazines like Glamour or Cosmopolitan often focus on new sex positions to try and embarrassing dates, O's coverage tends to appeal to an older crowd. Recent articles discussed how tea helps lower blood pressure and offered advice on how to talk to a doctor about medical history. Beth Babyak, a 40-year-old Oprah fan who was attending her second conference, said she did not subscribe to the magazine.

"I find it still skews older," Ms. Babyak said. When she does read it, she added, "I skip through sections."

Ms. Winfrey has been reaching some younger women through former talk show guests turned magazine contributors. Heather Hooke, 27, and her sister, Summer Swindell, 32, both subscribers, attended the conference because they like certain speakers who used to appear on

Ms. Winfrey's show, like Martha Beck, a life coach who recently wrote columns about managing anxiety and being more decisive. Ms. Swindell also follows the sex columnist Dr. Laura Berman, who appears on Ms. Winfrey's radio network. Both Ms. Hooke and Ms. Swindell seemed to view Ms. Winfrey as a maternal figure who shepherds this self-help flock.

"She's like the mother of every mother," Ms. Swindell said.

When Ms. Winfrey started the magazine a dozen years ago, it broadened her audience to include more affluent and educated readers than viewers of her TV program. (An issue costs $4.50 on newsstands.) And that initially paid off. Ms. Peck said the magazine's debut in April 2000 was one of the most financially successful in the industry's history. Readers devoured musings from Ms. Winfrey and columns written by talk show guests like Dr. Phil McGraw and Suze Orman. Ms. Orman called contributing to the magazine and attending the conference vital to her work because of the exposure she gets to her fans.

"I've written for Oprah's magazine since Day 1," Ms. Orman said after taking refuge from the hordes of fans who followed her from a book signing at the conference at a Jenny Craig booth, which was waiting for another guest, Valerie Bertinelli. "I wrote for the magazine so it would bring people into my life."

While its circulation and advertising clearly benefited from the talk show's popularity, Ms. King, the magazine's editor at large, said that Ms. Winfrey never let the magazine depend too heavily on the program to drive sales.

"We always thought there was something in the magazine that could be promoted on the show, at least once a month. But Oprah didn't feel that way," Ms. King said. "That's just not how she rolls, as the kids say."

Hearst executives were also prepared for sales to take a hit once the show ended. Susan Casey, the magazine's editor in chief since 2010, said that some readers thought when the talk show ended, the magazine was folding as well. But that confusion seems to have passed, and the magazine is attracting attention to itself by collaborating with other parts of Ms. Winfrey's empire. It coordinated with OWN to produce "Oprah's Favorite Things" episode that was broadcast on Nov. 18 and featured items appearing in O's December issue, which included high-end items like a $1,440 electric bike. The July issue highlighted Ms. Winfrey's pick for her revived book club.

Ms. Winfrey is confident she will draw more younger fans because people want "what we have to say in this magazine about fulfilling your destiny, who you're meant to be, living your best life." That's the kind of product Ms. Winfrey predicts people, regardless of age, will continue to pay for.

"You're never going to run out of people who are looking for a more joyful life," she said. Some of the answers to Ms. Winfrey's quest for a younger audience may simply be bridged by her original fans. Lynne Shewan, 56, a retired special education teacher from East Setauket, N.Y., attended the conference to get the advice from Ms. Winfrey she has been missing since the show ended. She said that she kept her magazine subscription and liked the columnists and updates about Ms. Winfrey. She watches Ms. Winfrey's "Lifeclass" show on OWN for her television fix.

"The magazine certainly isn't a replacement for the show," Ms. Shewan said.

Ms. Shewan noted that the conference gave Ms. Winfrey one new convert. Ms. Shewan invited her 24-year-old daughter, Briana, who initially laughed at the offer, calling the gathering "the Oprah convention."

But throughout the day, Briana Shewan's opinions changed.

"I was more into it than I thought I would be," Ms. Shewan said.

The question for Hearst and Ms. Winfrey is whether there are enough of those younger readers waiting to embrace O's message.

"For sure Hearst wants to make some money," Ms. Winfrey said. "You know, every time I get a check from it, it's like 'Wow, this is amazing. I get paid for doing this.' "

Winfrey Gives $12 Million to New Smithsonian Museum of Black History and Culture

BY GRAHAM BOWLEY | JUNE 12, 2013

OPRAH WINFREY IS giving $12 million to help build the Smithsonian's National Museum of African American History and Culture in Washington, the museum announced on Tuesday.

Due to open in late 2015, the planned $500 million museum is being constructed on a five-acre site next to the Washington Monument on the National Mall.

In recognition of Ms. Winfrey's gift, the museum's 350-seat theater, one of the building's largest spaces, is to be named the Oprah Winfrey Theater.

"The theater's programs will enable audiences to gain a broader understanding of how African American history and culture shape and enrich the country and the world," the Smithsonian said in a statement. It said the "theater will be a forum in the nation's capital for performers, artists, educators, scholars, authors, musicians, filmmakers and opinion leaders."

"This gift helps us get to the finishing line in terms of construction," said Lonnie G. Bunch III, the museum's director, in an interview. "Oprah has also given her imprimatur and that helps with fundraising and visibility."

So far the museum has raised $335 million toward the $500 million cost of design, construction and exhibitions, including $145 million from private sources, he said.

Other large donors include the Gates Foundation and the Lilly Endowment, which have each given $10 million.

Mr. Bunch said the building, now under construction and designed by the team of Freelon Adjaye Bond/SmithGroup to evoke the art of an ancient West African kingdom — should be finished in one and a half to two years. "We are on track and on budget," he said. Despite cutbacks in Washington, he said, congressional financing had been forthcoming. "We are grateful. We have done well."

Together with $1 million she gave in 2007, Ms. Winfrey's latest gift means she is now the single largest donor to date, the museum said. She has been a member of the museum's advisory council since 2004; other council members include Richard D. Parsons, former chairman of Citigroup, and Laura W. Bush.

"By investing in this museum, I want to help ensure that we both honor and preserve our culture and history, so that the stories of who we are will live on for generations to come," Ms. Winfrey said in the official statement.

The museum was established as a Smithsonian museum by an act of Congress in 2003.

The Tao of Oprah

BY JENNIFER CONLIN | OCT. 10, 2014

THERE IS A MOMENT halfway through Oprah Winfrey's "The Life You Want Weekend" when you wonder if you will ever actually see Oprah. Or if you still want to.

Don't get me wrong; she is everywhere. At least in O Town — the pop-up theme park village of hospitality tents, set up in all eight cities she is touring this fall. But it is Faux-prah — not her full-bodied self — that greets the thousands of women who pour into these outdoor marketplaces, always situated a short walking distance from where she and her self-help "trailblazers" ultimately speak.

"Quick, let's take a picture with her and post it on Facebook," said one woman who arrived at the Detroit O Town on a cloudy Friday morning last month. I whipped my head around looking for Oprah, only to see the woman race off with her friend to a life-size version of Oprah on a large screen filled with the tour's logo — an orange-and-yellow rainbow, signifying the renewal and energy of a sunrise. A willing stranger snapped their picture as they mimicked Oprah's stance in the photo — arms wide open to the world, mouths wide open with glee.

"Posted!" she announced to her friend before they ran off to see the "Oprah Winfrey Show Gallery," a board filled with framed photos of the TV host interviewing stars like Barbra Streisand and Barbara Walters.

This fall, Oprah Winfrey has been touring the United States with a series of these "The Life You Want" weekends, in cities like Newark, Houston, Miami and Seattle, drawing streams of people who continue to see Ms. Winfrey as a spiritual guru, and now, with her daily talk show having gone off the air in 2011, have come in search of what they have been missing.

I had come to Auburn Hills, a suburb of Detroit not far from where I live, with my friend Achla on what was the second stop of this tour, after Atlanta. And though neither of us are exactly Oprah fanatics, we

Oprah Winfrey on stage at her "The Life You Want Weekend" at the Prudential Center in Newark, N.J.

were fans of her show — and of her — and were beginning to get in the spirit of the thing.

Achla wanted us to "post" too. An hour later, while standing with a group of women in the O Magazine Lounge admiring a wall covered with glossy Oprah covers, I announced to my new friends that I already had 29 Facebook "likes" on my Oprah photo. Everyone cheered.

"Would you like to join Oprah's Circle of Friends?" a woman in a yellow sunrise Oprah shirt asked Achla and me, explaining that it is a tiered magazine subscription/fan club that for $199 gets you, among other things, a birthday card personally sent by Oprah.

"Do we get to meet Gayle?" Achla asked, referring to Oprah's best friend, Gayle King. "No," we were told, but the woman added that Ms. King would be making an appearance at O Town later in the weekend. (True, as I later found out when her bodyguard stopped me in my tracks when I inadvertently came close to knocking her down.)

Looking around it was hard to decide where to go next — the Toyota tent, where we could decorate a free journal at a craft table, the Olay tent, where we could get a makeover, or the Ikea tent, where we could learn how to make our home "a sanctuary."

Feeling tired — O Town in Detroit was a coffee-free zone, unfortunately — we headed to the Reinvention Tent, where we quickly met some people filling in the end of the sentence "I bring it by …" on a whiteboard wall. As I looked at what others had written — "Paying attention," "Staying connected," "Loving others" — I turned and found next to me a man contemplating his answer, an exotic sight in the heavily female O Town.

"I am here because my wife put a gun to my head," he deadpanned.

Waiting for a Pantene-sponsored head massage, I met Pamela McCoy, 65, a retired nurse. "I am just so excited to be here," she said, though she admitted to being slightly annoyed that her two working daughters could not join her until 7 that night, when Oprah would finally take the stage. "There is so much to do here and so many people to meet," she said enthusiastically, excited about the packed schedule of events taking place outside on the O Town stage — yoga sessions, cooking demonstrations and a fashion show featuring University of Michigan cheerleaders.

In a 45-minute-long line, where one could win a $999 V.I.P. upgrade, we met Evelyn Oja, 54, the mother of three 20-something boys all still living at home. "I came alone, wanting to become a calmer person," said Ms. Oja, who said she has been a huge Oprah fan ever since she first watched her show on "A.M. Chicago" in the mid-'80s.

"If I wanted a girl's weekend, I would have gone shopping with my friends," she added, obviously not yet aware of how much shopping was actually taking place all around her.

In the nearby Oprah shop, women were whipping out their credit cards to buy Oprah's book "What I Know for Sure" ($25), as well as "Oprah's Soul Library" (five bundled paperbacks for $79), not to mention the T-shirts ($38), hoodies ($60) and phone covers ($20), all branded with Oprah's big "O" signature, alongside a peace and love sign.

Meanwhile, my friend Achla was getting cranky. Not only did we not win the V.I.P. upgrade, which would have gotten us floor seats for that night and access to special V.I.P. tent lines (kind of like Disney's FastPass), but the freebies were scarce.

"Where's the free car?" Achla asked, remembering the 2004 TV show in which Oprah gave everyone in the audience a brand new Pontiac G6. I pointed out that there was indeed a car in the Toyota-sponsored tent, where she could have her picture taken, and that we had indeed received both a travel-size tube of Crest and a small bag of Tide capsules in the Reinvention tent, but that did not help.

It turned out we were not the only ones feeling anger over the disorganization and dollar signs. "I did not come all this way to stand in lines," said Jeanine Smith, who had flown to Detroit from North Carolina to meet her sister and mother who live in Chicago (the family estimated that the cost of the weekend, with hotel, flights, food and transportation, was totaling $2,000).

"I wonder how much you have to pay to not have to pay for stuff?" asked Erica Hobbs, 30, who had bought a ticket for $199. "I came here to be spiritual, not commercial," she added.

Like us, most women ended up leaving O Town after a couple of hours and heading to the nearby super-mall, where we could all do some real shopping and bonding (our plastic Oprah wristbands made it easy to identify one another in the stores).

But that night, everything changed. And not just because the two women from Ohio sitting next to me generously gave me one of the four glasses of chardonnay they had bought at the concession stand just before the show started. It was because the moment had finally come: to see Oprah … not on TV, not on the cover of a magazine or a book, not on her OWN network, but in person.

When the lights went dark, everyone's cheering immediately subsided. Oprah's voice started booming through the arena, but like the Wizard of Oz behind the curtain, she was still not visible. "In the words of Carl Sagan," she said, "we are made of star stuff." Our wristbands

The weekend included appearances by, from left, Iyanla Vanzant, Rob Bell, Elizabeth Gilbert and Mark Nepo.

suddenly lit up a bright white. It was as if she had the power to turn the room and us into one big constellation.

"We love you Oprah!" people started shouting. And then just as her soothing voice reminded us that "No matter how dark it gets on the hills, the sun will always rise," she rose, on some sort of elevator complete with stairs that she then walked down onto the stage to join us. With our wristbands now glowing orange to reflect the sun and her full-length gown a shimmering green, people jumped to their feet evangelically clapping wildly.

"You came! You're here!" she shouted out to us. "Why are you here?" she continued, calming us down. "I don't sing or dance, and Stedman said to tell you I don't have a hit record," she said teasingly, referring to her boyfriend, Stedman Graham. Considering that the last time I had been at this arena, which has a capacity of 20,000, was to see a sold-out Coldplay concert, I had to stop and think. But then she answered the question for us, "I am here to help you figure out why you are here." Later, she would admit that even Oprah sometimes needs Oprah's help. "Now and then I listen to a tape of what I have said to take my own advice," she told us. I wondered if she had to pay for that.

For the next two hours, Oprah revealed herself to us under a Jumbotron screen of serenity — images of an oak grove where she likes to sit and think, of water flowing over rocks, and sunrises coming up over horizons. Punctuating her story about being an unwanted child, getting pregnant at 14, breaking into television at 19 and changing her show to be a force of good, not evil, in the late '80s, she told us stories about Stevie Wonder, Maya Angelou, Steven Spielberg and Mr. Graham. "Stedman told me I am not a nice person, but that Gayle is," she said, making us laugh alongside her.

And though she shared her favorite inspirational quotes from Martin Luther King Jr. and Pierre Teilhard de Chardin, among others, it was Oprah's catchphrases — "You are the master of your fate," "You are responsible for the energy you bring into your space," "Whatever has happened to you has happened for you" — that had the crowd clapping, waving, crying and hugging. Finally, around 9 p.m., she sent us home like schoolchildren, instructing us to "get ready to use our power" the next morning, when we were all due back at 9.

As I walked out with my new girlfriends from Ohio, one of them said: "I feel like we were in a living room, not a concert hall, tonight. It really feels like she is your friend." I had to agree, though others felt less girl-friendly about Oprah.

"I don't worship at the altar of Oprah, so I found it rather strange that people around me were chanting," said Nadine Hall, 46, a teacher, who came only because she was given a free ticket that day. "But I am probably not her target audience. I don't need to find purpose or repurpose in my life right now. I am actually quite happy." I wondered if she would be bored the next day.

When we returned Saturday morning, the arena had a completely different feel from the previous night. With the lights now up and our wristbands turned off, you could see the seats were only a bit more than half full. Gone was Oprah's gown, replaced with work clothes — blue-jeans, a red twin set and red glasses to match (that afternoon she would change into a turquoise top with yet another pair of matching glasses).

Now we held workbooks in our hands for the three Oprah-led workshops we would experience that day, and it was clear that it was time to get serious. And we did, first by writing a paragraph on what we wish for someone we love (spoiler alert — it turns out to be you); then filling out a pie chart of our lives with happy and sad faces ("This can't be good," Achla said to me, giving me a peek at her circle full of frowns); and finally creating a vision for our future — something we did not have to do that day but were meant to work on in the future. I tried to vision, visioning.

"One of the reasons I stepped off the show," Oprah confided in us, "is because the only thing I was really interested in talking about is what we are talking about today," adding later, "I am here to help you turn up the volume in your life" — which appeared to work, particularly in the afternoon, when an impromptu conga line took place on the floor.

In between the workshops, we heard from Oprah's trailblazers. Mark Nepo's meditation nearly put me to sleep, but Elizabeth Gilbert of "Eat, Pray, Love" fame, perked me up with her perkiness immediately. She urged us to become the heroes of our own stories (something she certainly conquered when Julia Roberts played her), then Iyanla Vanzant, the biggest star besides Oprah on OWN, told us to get rid of the "humping puppies" (the negative voices in our heads) while sipping Champagne (it was her birthday, and we all sang to her).

After various breaks (including an arena-wide group SoulCycle session) and a lengthy lunch (where everyone complained about the cost and quality of the food, including the $15 pre-ordered Oprah box lunch, which contained only half a sandwich, an apple, a bag of chips and water), I felt as if I had been at a weeklong slumber party — tired and emotional and ready to go home.

Oprah, however, still seemed ready to go. Turns out she had even gone out to the parking lot for a mimosa with a group of tailgating women. "All of a sudden she climbed out of a black car and was taking pictures with us," said Patty Waynick, 48, who, unlike me, had been able to get close enough to Gayle to make the request that Oprah visit their group.

Wondering whether anyone had actually found the "life they wanted" over the weekend, I decided to contact a few of my new friends. Jen Muse, 42, an architect from Ohio who had sat next to me, said: "I wish I had a super 'aha' that made me realize how to live my best life, but it's just not that easy. But what I did take away is that all the stresses and trials are O.K. They are part of my journey."

And though Erica Hobbs and Jeanine Smith had both found the consumerism distasteful, the speakers seemed to have made them forget the expense. "I believe what Oprah says, that we are the masters of our fate," said Ms. Smith, a music composer. "Life is not serendipity but opportunity, and you have to be prepared for it when it comes your way and align it."

"I was totally blown away," said Ms. Hobbs, who initially bought her ticket just to hear Ms. Gilbert speak. "I am now completely on the Oprah bandwagon."

"To see her in person, with her presence and energy, cannot be replicated," she added. "She is a force out there."

Even Ms. Hall, who seemed to need Oprah the least of anyone in the audience, said she couldn't help but admire what she was achieving on the tour. "She creates a safe, comfortable atmosphere for women where they can be emotional," Ms. Hall said. "I have never seen so many friendly women in one place."

Perhaps Oprah's parting words also helped. "Thank you for your money," she said, shortly before bidding her devotees goodbye. "I know how hard you all work."

And then, on my way out, I somehow found I couldn't help myself any longer. I went and bought her book and one of her $60 hoodies.

Oprah 2020? Democrats Swing From Giddy to Skeptical at the Prospect

BY ALEXANDER BURNS AND AMY CHOZICK | JAN. 8, 2018

WASHINGTON — With a booming speech at the Golden Globe Awards on Sunday night, Oprah Winfrey, the billionaire media entrepreneur and former television talk-show host, launched a thousand fantasies for Democrats: Of a historic campaign to put a black woman in the White House. Of a celebrity candidate, known for her big-hearted optimism, taking on a reality-show president defined by his thirst for combat. Of a presidency, some joked, where everybody would get a car.

Ms. Winfrey's longtime partner, Stedman Graham, stoked the mood in a newspaper interview, suggesting to The Los Angeles Times that she would "absolutely do it" — with the caveat that such matters are "up to the people."

There was no more official signal on Monday from Ms. Winfrey, 63, as to her interest in the presidency. She has disavowed any ambition to be a candidate in the past, though she has told associates in recent months that she wants to play a part in bringing the country together, two people briefed on her thinking said.

If Ms. Winfrey's ambitions are unclear, the sometimes giddy reaction to her speech at a Hollywood awards dinner underscored the unfulfilled hunger among Democrats for a larger-than-life leader to challenge President Trump.

With no obvious front-runner for the 2020 campaign, Democrats appear likely to spend the next few years grinding through internal disagreements over policy and identity in a long contest for the nomination. There are thorny disagreements in the party about how bluntly liberal its agenda should be, how boldly to confront Mr. Trump and how to balance the task of turning out core Democratic voters with the desire to win over disaffected Republicans and independents.

In the imagination of some Democrats, Ms. Winfrey might offer an easy way out of those problems. She inspires crucial groups for the party — women and African-Americans — and alienates few. She has cast herself in American culture as an avatar of optimism, not defined in ideological terms. Having made a career out of preaching the values of empowerment and inclusion, she represents in some ways a natural counterpoint to Mr. Trump's proud pugilism. Senior Democrats in Washington said on Monday they had received no signal from Ms. Winfrey that she hoped to seek the White House.

David Axelrod, the former chief strategist for Barack Obama, said Ms. Winfrey was a figure of unique political potential, with "a boundless capacity for empathy and a preternatural ability to communicate powerfully and authentically — as we saw at the Golden Globes."

Mr. Axelrod questioned, however, whether Ms. Winfrey would be the right fit for 2020: "Would she want to submit herself to the unforgiving, relentless and sometimes absurd process of running for president?" he wondered, adding: "Will there be hunger in 2020 for someone with some experience in government, after Trump?"

Some Democrats expressed skepticism and even frustration about the swirl of fascination with Ms. Winfrey, arguing that the party was jumping the gun with fevered speculation about 2020. Senator Brian Schatz of Hawaii, a young liberal in the chamber, wrote tersely on Twitter: "Hey. Let's focus on winning in 2018. Thanks."

Rebecca Katz, a Democratic strategist from the party's progressive wing, said it would be a mistake for Democrats to rush toward a magnetic personality rather than hashing out a compelling agenda for the midterm elections and beyond.

"Beating Trump isn't just about finding the right candidate — we have to show what we stand for," Ms. Katz said. "Other than 'we all get a car,' what will an Oprah presidency look like?" she added, referring to when Ms. Winfrey famously gave a car to every audience member at her show.

Ms. Winfrey's sudden prominence in the nation's political imagination speaks, in some respects, to the merging of politics and entertainment in the American mind. She has occupied a singular role in the television industry, parlaying roles as a local news anchor and a talk-show host in Chicago into a media empire that includes her own cable network and a fortune estimated at close to $3 billion. Gallup polling regularly finds Ms. Winfrey among the country's most admired women, alongside Hillary Clinton and Michelle Obama.

Representative Nancy Pelosi of California, the House Democratic leader, suggested — with a dose of skepticism — that Ms. Winfrey was the kind of political outsider Democrats might embrace.

Alluding to Mr. Trump's lack of experience, Ms. Pelosi tartly told a small group of reporters that Ms. Winfrey had other qualities going for her: "Oprah has read books. She knows how to identify talent."

"If we're going into a place where they are devaluing experience in terms of substance and legislative acumen and stuff like that," Ms. Pelosi said, "you might as well have somebody who knows what they don't know and would get the best possible people there."

Ms. Winfrey's commercial reach transcends race and income level, analysts say, propelling so many books and products to overnight success that it has earned its own sobriquet: "The Oprah Effect." In 2015, Ms. Winfrey bought a 10 percent stake in Weight Watchers and assumed a position on the company's board, a move that instantly doubled the company's sluggish share price and added $400 million to its market value.

Other investments have eluded that Midas touch. Ms. Winfrey's cable channel, OWN: The Oprah Winfrey Network, a joint venture with Discovery Communications Inc., initially struggled to gain traction and last year earned an average of 462,000 prime time viewers daily. In December, Discovery said it would take majority control of OWN, purchasing 24.5 percent of the channel for $70 million from Ms. Winfrey's company, Harpo.

Ms. Winfrey's most potent appeal, industry analysts say, is among somewhat older consumers — or perhaps, voters — with women over 55 as her strongest cohort. She is especially popular among African-American women and white suburban women, two groups Democrats will rely on in the 2018 and 2020 elections.

By Monday afternoon, the White House had responded to the threat of Oprah in 2020. "We welcome the challenge," said Hogan Gidley, a spokesman for the president, "whether it be Oprah Winfrey or anybody else."

But Ms. Winfrey has approached politics cautiously over the years, engaging highly selectively. In 2007, she intervened for Mr. Obama, holding rallies for him and hailing him as "the one." And in 2013, she hosted a fund-raising event for Cory Booker, in his first bid for Senate in New Jersey.

During the 2016 campaign, Ms. Winfrey endorsed Mrs. Clinton but never ventured onto the campaign trail. Though Ms. Winfrey and her staff discussed a possible appearance with the Clinton campaign, none was ever scheduled. Ms. Winfrey's aides cited her focus on righting her television network as the reason for her difficult schedule.

Minyon Moore, a Clinton adviser who communicated with the Winfrey team, said the campaign had been "delighted" to have Ms. Winfrey's endorsement. Should Ms. Winfrey seek to assemble a campaign team for 2020, Ms. Moore said, "I suspect she would have her pick."

Less certain is whether Ms. Winfrey could navigate the ideological pitfalls of a presidential campaign and give voice not just to broad themes, but actual policy prescriptions. While Ms. Winfrey has aligned herself generally with Democrats like Mr. Obama, her views on a range of issues from financial regulation to drone warfare are opaque. She drew criticism from the left last year after saying in an interview that she felt hopeful and believed Mr. Trump had been "humbled" after meeting with Mr. Obama during the presidential transition.

Alixandria Lapp, a strategist helping lead Democrats' effort to retake the House, said the profile of a media mogul outsider would be an uncomfortable match for the party.

"I think it's highly unlikely that Democrats will ever nominate our own version of Donald Trump — a celebrity with no government experience — because our party tends to respect government and governing experience," Ms. Lapp said.

Ms. Winfrey has recently taken on political topics as a special correspondent for CBS News's "60 Minutes," including a segment on the country's political divisions and another on the use of solitary confinement in prisons.

But even to close friends and admirers, the prospect of an Oprah 2020 race appeared far-fetched or impossible as recently as last year. After Mr. Trump's inauguration, when the traditional barriers to entry into presidential politics appeared to melt away, Ms. Winfrey's associates dismissed the idea.

A reporter who last March contacted Ms. Winfrey's best friend, Gayle King of CBS News, got an emphatic reaction to the 2020 question.

"NOT A CHANCE!!!!!" Ms. King replied at the time, adding: "In caps for a reason."

THOMAS KAPLAN and **JONATHAN MARTIN** contributed reporting.

CHAPTER 3

Liberal Powerhouses: Warren Buffett and George Soros

Few billionaires have attracted as much media attention as Warren Buffett and George Soros. Buffett, the founder of Berkshire Hathaway, has become an outspoken proponent of liberal politicians and has famously pledged the bulk of his wealth to philanthropic organizations. George Soros has also made a name for himself as a major contributor to charitable and liberal causes. In this chapter, the articles show the background of these two investors as well as the scrutiny they face.

Buffett to Give Bulk of His Fortune to Gates Charity

BY TIMOTHY L. O'BRIEN AND STEPHANIE SAUL | JUNE 26, 2006

WARREN E. BUFFETT, the chairman of Berkshire Hathaway Inc. and one of the world's wealthiest men, plans to donate the bulk of his $44 billion fortune to the Bill & Melinda Gates Foundation and four other philanthropies starting in July.

The donations, outlined in a series of letters that Mr. Buffett released yesterday and will execute today, represent a singular and historic act of charitable giving that vaults him into the top tier of industrialists and entrepreneurs like Andrew Carnegie, John D. Rockefeller Sr., Henry Ford, J. Paul Getty, W. K. Kellogg and Mr. Gates himself, all men whose fortunes have endowed some of the world's richest private foundations.

Mr. Buffett plans to give away 85 percent of his fortune, or about $37.4 billion, all in Berkshire stock. Of that amount, he will channel the greatest share, about $31 billion, into the Gates Foundation. The Gates Foundation, dedicated to improving health and education, especially in poor nations, is already the United States' largest grant-making foundation, with current assets of almost $30 billion. Mr. Buffett's huge contribution may permanently solidify that philanthropy's standing as the biggest and most influential organization of its kind. Mr. Buffett will join Mr. and Mrs. Gates as a trustee of their foundation.

The immense size of the assets at the disposal of the Gates Foundation as a result of the partnership is apparent when compared with the United Nations Educational, Scientific and Cultural Organization, or Unesco, which had a budget of $610 million for 2004-05. The Gates Foundation made $1.36 billion in grant payments in 2005; at a minimum, Mr. Buffett's contribution may eventually allow the foundation to more than double that amount annually once he transfers all of his stock.

Mr. Buffett's contribution will not be made all at once, but rather in smaller annual increments. Moreover, the distribution could change in an as-yet unspecified way if Mr. Buffett dies before the entire sum is paid. The terms of the donation also require the continued active participation of at least one of the Gateses for the payments to continue.

The second-largest charitable foundation in the country is the Ford Foundation, with an endowment of $11.6 billion.

Mr. Buffett, 75, and Mr. Gates, 50, have become extremely close business associates and confidants since they met in 1991, and the linking of their fortunes and their legacies through the Gates Foundation marks the latest twist in their friendship. In addition to traveling together and regularly playing online bridge games, the two men routinely seek out each other's advice on personal and business matters.

The formation of the charitable partnership between the Gateses and Mr. Buffett was accompanied by a publicity campaign that was hard to ignore, starting with a full-page advertisement today in The New York Times about a joint interview with Charlie Rose that will be broadcast on PBS tonight.

Today's joint public appearances were to begin with what was billed as a "chat" between the philanthropists at the New York Public Library at 11 a.m., followed by a one-hour news conference at a Manhattan hotel.

Mr. Gates, who announced about two weeks ago that he planned to devote less of his time to his role as Microsoft chairman starting in 2008 so he could focus on his foundation, joined Berkshire's board of directors last year. Mr. Buffett is a Microsoft investor through Berkshire, and Mr. Gates said early last year that he personally owned about $300 million worth of Berkshire stock.

Gene Tempel, executive director of the Center on Philanthropy at Indiana University, said, "I'm not sure anytime in history we've ever seen someone give away a sum of money that large to another foundation," referring to Mr. Buffett's donation to the Gates Foundation. "Most people with this sum of money would try to create their own foundation in their own image; he's entrusting it to someone with whom he's had a good close relationship but who is 25 years his junior, who might be around to make sure it is used properly."

Details about Mr. Buffett's donations were first disclosed yesterday online at Fortune.com. They will also be outlined in a Fortune magazine cover article in its July 10th issue.

Mr. Buffett had insisted that he would wait until his death to make a sizable charitable bequest, but he told Fortune that the death of his wife, Susan, in 2004, his admiration for the Gateses and his certainty about how to dispose of his wealth had caused him to "get going" now.

The donation from Mr. Buffett "continues to increase the size of the Gates Foundation and the size and scope of the projects they can undertake," Mr. Tempel said. "They will have organizational challenges in determining how they manage that, how they create the kind of partnerships and staffing that can carry out the work."

The other charities that Mr. Buffett will divide about $6 billion in stock among are the Susan Thompson Buffett Foundation, which is named after Mr. Buffett's wife and emphasizes family planning, abortion rights and anti-nuclear proliferation issues; the Howard G. Buffett Foundation, which is named after and run by one of Mr. Buffett's two sons and focuses on environmental and conservation issues; the Susan A. Buffett Foundation, which is named after and run by Mr. Buffett's daughter and supports educational opportunities for low-income children; and the NoVo Foundation, which is run by Mr. Buffett's other son, Peter Buffett, and has focused on education and human rights.

Over the last four decades, Mr. Buffett has built Berkshire, which is based in Omaha, into one of the world's largest and most successful insurers. Along the way, he has also assembled a stable of holdings in well-known media, consumer products and energy concerns; navigated the stock market with legendary prowess; and offered folksy, astute guidelines for proper corporate governance and investment savvy.

One of his companies, the General Re Corporation, is the subject of a continuing federal investigation into possible financial crimes. Mr. Buffett has not been accused of any wrongdoing in the matter.

In his letters yesterday to the Gates Foundation and the four other beneficiaries, Mr. Buffett said that he had talented managers waiting to succeed him and that the Berkshire shares were "an ideal asset to underpin the long-term well-being of a foundation" because his company had "a multitude of diversified and powerful streams of earnings, Gibraltar-like financial strength, and a deeply-imbedded culture of acting in the best interests of shareholders."

Fred P. Hochberg, dean of the Milano School for Management and Urban Policy at the New School, which has a large nonprofit-management department, said Mr. Buffett's historic contribution to the Gates Foundation was in character.

"It's egoless," he said. "Warren's name is not on the door."

Buy American. I Am.

OPINION | BY WARREN E. BUFFETT | OCT. 16, 2008

THE FINANCIAL WORLD is a mess, both in the United States and abroad. Its problems, moreover, have been leaking into the general economy, and the leaks are now turning into a gusher. In the near term, unemployment will rise, business activity will falter and headlines will continue to be scary.

So ... I've been buying American stocks. This is my personal account I'm talking about, in which I previously owned nothing but United States government bonds. (This description leaves aside my Berkshire Hathaway holdings, which are all committed to philanthropy.) If prices keep looking attractive, my non-Berkshire net worth will soon be 100 percent in United States equities.

Why?

A simple rule dictates my buying: Be fearful when others are greedy, and be greedy when others are fearful. And most certainly, fear is now widespread, gripping even seasoned investors. To be sure, investors are right to be wary of highly leveraged entities or businesses in weak competitive positions. But fears regarding the long-term prosperity of the nation's many sound companies make no sense. These businesses will indeed suffer earnings hiccups, as they always have. But most major companies will be setting new profit records 5, 10 and 20 years from now.

Let me be clear on one point: I can't predict the short-term movements of the stock market. I haven't the faintest idea as to whether stocks will be higher or lower a month — or a year — from now. What is likely, however, is that the market will move higher, perhaps substantially so, well before either sentiment or the economy turns up. So if you wait for the robins, spring will be over.

A little history here: During the Depression, the Dow hit its low, 41, on July 8, 1932. Economic conditions, though, kept deteriorating until Franklin D. Roosevelt took office in March 1933. By that time, the market had already advanced 30 percent. Or think back to the early days of World War II, when things were going badly for the United States in Europe and the Pacific. The market hit bottom in April 1942, well before Allied fortunes turned. Again, in the early 1980s, the time to buy stocks was when inflation raged and the economy was in the tank. In short, bad news is an investor's best friend. It lets you buy a slice of America's future at a marked-down price.

Over the long term, the stock market news will be good. In the 20th century, the United States endured two world wars and other traumatic and expensive military conflicts; the Depression; a dozen or so recessions and financial panics; oil shocks; a flu epidemic; and the resignation of a disgraced president. Yet the Dow rose from 66 to 11,497.

You might think it would have been impossible for an investor to lose money during a century marked by such an extraordinary gain. But some investors did. The hapless ones bought stocks only when they felt comfort in doing so and then proceeded to sell when the headlines made them queasy.

Today people who hold cash equivalents feel comfortable. They shouldn't. They have opted for a terrible long-term asset, one that pays virtually nothing and is certain to depreciate in value. Indeed, the policies that government will follow in its efforts to alleviate the current crisis will probably prove inflationary and therefore accelerate declines in the real value of cash accounts.

Equities will almost certainly outperform cash over the next decade, probably by a substantial degree. Those investors who cling now to cash are betting they can efficiently time their move away from it later. In waiting for the comfort of good news, they are ignoring Wayne Gretzky's advice: "I skate to where the puck is going to be, not to where it has been."

I don't like to opine on the stock market, and again I emphasize that I have no idea what the market will do in the short term. Nevertheless, I'll follow the lead of a restaurant that opened in an empty bank building and then advertised: "Put your mouth where your money was." Today my money and my mouth both say equities.

WARREN E. BUFFETT is the chief executive of Berkshire Hathaway, a diversified holding company.

America's Billionaire

OPINION | BY MAUREEN DOWD | SEPT. 21, 2013

WASHINGTON — When you're trapped in a city with House Republican gargoyles who don't understand math or history, much less reality, sometimes you crave a dose of grandfatherly wisdom.

Speaker John Boehner, trapped under the thumb of Tea Party anarchists, called Friday's vote to defund Obamacare and invite a government shutdown, "a victory for common sense."

More like a triumph of nonsense.

The victory for common sense last week was not in Congress, but at Georgetown University. Speaking to an excited crowd of students and others Thursday night beneath soaring stained-glass windows, the 83-year-old Warren Buffett offered inspiring lessons in patriotism and compassion — traits sorely missing here as Republicans ran headlong toward a global economic cataclysm and gutted the food stamp program.

"I am sorry I'm late," Nancy Pelosi murmured sardonically, as she arrived at the Buffett event. "We were busy taking food out of the mouths of babies."

Questioned by Brian Moynihan, the C.E.O. of Bank of America, and later students, Buffett seemed happy to be back in one of his home-towns, where, as the son of an investor from Omaha who became a congressman, he had once worked as a waterboy for the Redskins and a paperboy for Georgetown Hospital.

His taste for making money was whetted when his customers at the hospital would give him bet suggestions for the numbers racket, big in Washington in those days.

"They would tell me if there was a woman that had given birth to a baby that was, say, 8 pounds, 11 ounces," he said, or the time of the birth.

The C.E.O. of Berkshire Hathaway said he began investing at age 11 in 1942, a couple months after Pearl Harbor, after spending five years saving up $120.

Warren Buffett, left, with Bank of America C.E.O. Brian Moynihan at Georgetown University this past Thursday.

He even joked that he had fond thoughts of 1929 because it was when he was conceived: "my dad was a stock salesman and after the crash he didn't have anything to do."

I wrote about Buffett in 1996, when Ted Turner upbraided fellow billionaires like Buffett and Bill Gates as "ol' skinflints" for not loosening up "their wads" because they were afraid to fall off the Forbes 400 List. Back then, Buffett said he would wait until after he and his wife died, when he planned to give the bulk of his $15 billion to population control (even though, of course, every moment counts on that cause).

But then, about five years ago, Buffett said at Georgetown, he and Gates began plotting about philanthropy and now they have enrolled 115 plutocrats pledging a majority of their net worth.

"I've been dialing for dollars," he said, adding that when billionaires resist, he gives them a warning: "If I'm talking to some 70-year-old, I say, 'Do you really think your decision-making ability is going to be better when you're 95 with some blonde on your lap, or now?' "

He calls the Fed "the greatest hedge fund in history," and observed of the moment America nearly went off the cliff: "I give enormous credit to Ben Bernanke and Hank Paulson and Tim Geithner and frankly, even though I didn't vote for him, President Bush."

W.'s "great insight," one worthy of Adam Smith, he said, was expressed in 10 words in September 2008: "He went out there from the White House and he said, 'If money doesn't loosen up this sucker could go down.' "

The populist voice of the 1 percent stressed that "inequality is getting wider" and that we must figure out how to "share the bounty."

"We've got something that works and we don't want to mess that up," he said. There will be periodic recessions and the occasional panic, he noted, advising that those times are good to buy stock at "silly prices."

"It's very hard to write regulations that will keep people from acting foolishly, particularly when acting foolishly has proven very profitable over the preceding few years," he said. "Humans, they all think they're Cinderella at the ball, and they think, as the night goes along, the music gets better and the drinks flow, they all think they're going to leave at two minutes to 12 and of course there's no clocks on the wall and they're still dancing, so it will happen again."

"But," he added slyly, "buy when it happens."

He doesn't worry about keeping up with modern technology. He buys what he knows, like Coca-Cola, which he drank all evening. Evoking Ted Williams "waiting for the right pitch," he counseled that: "You don't need 20 decisions to get very rich. Four or five will probably do it over time."

Being a successful investor is not about having a high I.Q., he said, "but it does take a temperament that's willing to step up and actually act. I always tell people, if they're going in the investment business and you've got a 160 I.Q., sell 30 points to somebody else because you won't need it."

Or sell some to the House Republicans.

MAUREEN DOWD, winner of the 1999 Pulitzer Prize for distinguished commentary, became an Op-Ed columnist in 1995.

How Warren Buffett Does It

OPINION | BY JOE NOCERA | MARCH 3, 2015

FIFTY YEARS AGO, a young investor named Warren Buffett took control of a failing textile company, Berkshire Hathaway. "I found myself … invested in a terrible business about which I knew very little," Buffett relates in his annual letter to shareholders, which was released over the weekend. "I became the dog who caught the car."

Buffett describes his approach in those days as "cigar butt" investing; buying shares of troubled companies with underpriced stocks was "like picking up a discarded cigar butt that had one puff remaining in it," he writes. "Though the stub might be ugly and soggy, the puff would be free." He continues: "Most of my gains in those early years … came from investments in mediocre companies that traded at bargain prices."

But that approach had limits. It took Charlie Munger, the Los Angeles lawyer who has been his longtime sidekick, to show him that there was another way to win at the investing game: "Forget what you know about buying fair businesses at wonderful prices," Munger told him. "Instead, buy wonderful businesses at fair prices." Which is what Buffett's been doing ever since.

He has done it in two ways. First — and this is what he is renowned for — he has bought stock in some of the great American companies of our time, stock that he has held not just for years, but for decades. Second, he has turned Berkshire Hathaway into a true conglomerate, which owns not just stocks but entire companies. Although Berkshire's front office employs only 25 people, its companies have, in total, some 340,500 employees.

How successful has the Buffett-Munger approach been? In the 50 years since Buffett took over Berkshire, its stock has appreciated by 1,826,163 percent. That is an astounding number.

You would think, given Buffett's success, that more people would try to emulate his approach to investing. It is not as if he hasn't tried to explain how he does it. Every year, you can find a Buffett tutorial in his annual letter that the rest of us would do well to absorb — and practice.

In the current letter, for instance, he makes the case — which has been made many times before — that a diversified portfolio of stocks "that are bought over time and that are owned in a manner invoking only token fees and commissions" are less risky over the long term than other investment vehicles that are tied to the dollar. Clearly, that's been his approach. He then goes on to bemoan the fact that too many investors — both little guys and investment professionals — do things that add risk: "Active trading, attempts to 'time' market movements, inadequate diversification, the payment of high and unnecessary fees ... and the use of borrowed money can destroy the decent returns that a life-long owner of equities would otherwise enjoy."

Another thing about Buffett is that he has never gotten caught up in fads. He only buys businesses that he understands and can predict where the business will be in a decade. He teaches this point in the current letter with a discussion of the conglomerates that sprung up in the 1960s and became the hot stocks of the moment. Jimmy Ling, who ran one such company, LTV, used to say that he looked for acquisitions where "2 plus 2 equals 5."

LTV, as conceived by Ling, of course, ceased to exist decades ago (though the company would go through several transformations and bankruptcy court before shuttering its last vestige in 2002). "Never forget that 2 + 2 will always equal 4," writes Buffett. "And when someone tells you how old-fashioned that math is — zip up your wallet, take a vacation and come back in a few years to buy stocks at cheap prices."

If it's really this simple, why don't more people try to invest like Buffett? One reason, I think, is that sound investing — buying when others are selling, holding for the long term, avoiding the hot stocks — requires a stronger stomach than most people have. When a stock is plummeting, it takes a certain strength to buy even more instead of selling in a panic. Most of us lack the temperament required for smart investing. The fundamental equanimity required to be a great investor is a rare thing.

The second reason is that investing the Warren Buffett way is a lot more complicated than he makes it sound. Can you predict where a business will be in 10 years? Of course not. But he can — and does.

In a few months, the faithful will flock to Omaha to attend Berkshire's annual meeting — "Woodstock for capitalists," Buffett likes to call it. For six hours, Buffett and Munger will be on stage, before some 40,000 people, cracking wise, while making their investment decisions sound like simplicity itself.

But, in coming to pay their annual homage, the throngs will not be acknowledging the simplicity of Buffett's approach, but the genius behind it.

JOE NOCERA is an Op-Ed columnist for The New York Times.

Warren Buffett Holds Forth on Sharing the Wealth

BY ANDREW ROSS SORKIN | MAY 2, 2016

OMAHA — Priyanka Bodalia, a 24-year-old from Cincinnati who works in accounting, was roaming the convention center here where Berkshire Hathaway's annual meeting was taking place Saturday afternoon. She couldn't have been more excited to hear from Warren E. Buffett, the company's chief executive, and his partner, Charlie Munger, as well as to see the parade of boldface names that made the pilgrimage.

"All my friends are jealous that I'm here," she said, beaming, as she stood with her father near the Dairy Queen booth. "I took a snap of Bill Gates and they were, like, 'Are you kidding me? You're in the same room as Bill Gates!' "

Ms. Bodalia was hardly the exception among the 40,000 shareholders who had traveled here for what has become known as the Woodstock for Capitalists, an unabashed celebration of business, investing, innovation and entrepreneurship.

But she may be, increasingly, an exception among her generation. A poll released last week by the Harvard Institute of Politics found that among 18-to-29-year-olds, only 19 percent identified themselves as "capitalists," and only 42 percent said they "supported" capitalism. The number was slightly higher for those in the next age group, 34 to 49 years old, with 31 percent identifying as capitalists and 50 percent saying they supported capitalism.

In Nebraska, where Bernie Sanders beat Hillary Clinton by a wide margin in the Democratic caucuses, the juxtaposition between this weekend-long tribute to capitalism and the skepticism expressed by a generation that questions the very premise of the system, was stark.

It is an issue that Mr. Buffett said he was well aware of. "You should be questioning it at that age," he said in an interview. Mr. Buffett, perhaps surprisingly, spoke positively about Mr. Sanders —

who rails against income inequality and the corrupting influence of money, and he praised him for being "direct" and "authentic." But Mr. Buffett, a Hillary Clinton supporter, said Mr. Sanders's solutions "are very off base."

"We have a system that has built abundance," Mr. Buffett said, and yet he acknowledged that "it left too many people behind." His answer for the next generation: "The conclusion shouldn't be to kill the golden goose," he said. Instead, he said we "need to make more eggs" and "distribute them better."

That is a message that should translate broadly, but it is not often articulated or championed effectively by the business community.

Ms. Bodalia said that some of her friends — most likely the ones who were unimpressed that she had seen Mr. Gates, and who might have been captured by Harvard's poll numbers — would benefit from a visit to Omaha. Indeed, underneath all the talk about investing, mostly to a wealthy, older crowd, was a more profound message about the businesses that power much of the economy and spur employment. It's a message that perhaps could use a wider audience.

While Mr. Buffett and Mr. Munger mostly sidestepped questions about politics over the weekend (I was one of three journalists who posed questions to them, along with three analysts and some share-holders), they have long communicated a philosophy of about creating a fairer, better version of capitalism.

"Financiers are among those who do receive undeserved wealth and have caused envy," Mr. Munger said just two months ago at the Daily Journal annual meeting, a corporate gathering in Los Angeles. "We don't want a lot of undeserved wealth for doing nothing or acting counterproductively. Fixing undeserved wealth would be extraordinary."

Still, Mr. Munger, who unlike Mr. Buffett leans conservative, suggested that socialism could lead to much worse results. "People passionate about egality gave us the Soviet Union and all those murders, and Communist China and the starvation, and lovely North Korea. I am suspicious of all this passion that brings about such bad examples."

He added, "Inequality is the natural outcome of a successful, advancing civilization. What the hell is the guy at the top 1 percent to do? Is he the main problem? When you get rich, you finally realize how little power the rich really have — they will spend a lot and get practically nowhere."

That economic worldview runs counter to the one Mr. Sanders has traded on so successfully this primary season, the one so many young people seem to believe.

As for Mr. Buffett, he has mostly managed to avoid becoming a political target, in part because he is often described as a compassionate capitalist. He regularly criticizes Wall Street rent-seekers, supports raising taxes on the rich and promotes the earned-income tax credit, for example. And yet his critics say his folksy image is for show, citing his stakes in Goldman Sachs and Wells Fargo and his partnership with 3G Capital, a firm known for running an extremely lean organization. They also cite the wealth he has tied up in Berkshire, which itself is run to limit his tax bill, and his plans to give it all away to charity, so Uncle Sam won't be getting much.

I'm not so sure all those positions are at odds. But for a new generation entering the workplace that has reasonable questions about whether the current system gives them enough opportunity, studying the ideas of Mr. Buffett could at least provide another perspective.

"Twenty years from now, there'll be far more output per capita in the United States in real terms than there is now," Mr. Buffett said. "In 50 years, it'll be far more. No presidential candidate or president is going to end that. They can shape it in ways that are good or bad, but they can't end it."

Buffett Calls Trump's Bluff and Releases His Tax Data

BY PATRICIA COHEN | OCT. 10, 2016

WARREN E. BUFFETT is not running for president. But on Monday, Mr. Buffett, the billionaire investor, volunteered more detailed information about his income taxes than Donald J. Trump, the Republican nominee, ever has.

Mr. Buffett released the information after essentially being called out by Mr. Trump during Sunday night's presidential debate.

Acknowledging for the first time that he had avoided paying federal income taxes for years by claiming nearly a billion dollars in losses in 1995, Mr. Trump then tried to shift attention to his Democratic opponent, Hillary Clinton, accusing some of her wealthy supporters of exploiting tax laws to their own advantage.

"Many of her friends took bigger deductions," Mr. Trump said. "Warren Buffett took a massive deduction."

Actually, he did not.

"I have paid federal income tax every year since 1944," Mr. Buffett wrote in a letter released Monday.

"My 2015 return shows adjusted gross income of $11,563,931," he revealed. "My deductions totaled $5,477,694." About two-thirds of those represented charitable contributions, he said. Most of the rest were related to Mr. Buffett's state income tax payments.

Mr. Buffett, the chairman of Berkshire Hathaway and one of the richest men in the world, went on to say: "My federal income tax for the year was $1,845,557. Returns for previous years are of a similar nature in respect to contributions, deductions and tax rates."

Last year, Mr. Buffett paid about 16 percent of his reported income in federal income taxes.

"I have copies of all 72 of my returns," Mr. Buffett added, "and none uses a carry forward," the provision that allows taxpayers like Mr.

Trump to use losses from one year to avoid paying personal federal income taxes both on some previous tax returns and in future years.

Mr. Trump had previously claimed, without producing any evidence, that Mr. Buffett declared $873 million in losses.

As it turns out, the charitable contributions that Mr. Buffett did deduct from his income make up just a tiny portion of the more than $2.85 billion he donated to charity last year, he said. The reason is that the tax code limits the amount that an individual can claim in charitable deductions. Mr. Buffett, 86, has pledged to give most of his $65 billion fortune away.

By contrast, Mr. Trump's own charitable foundations — and his claims about his personal contributions — have come under scrutiny. Last week the New York attorney general ordered the Donald J. Trump Foundation to stop soliciting donations in the state because it lacked the required registration. And many of the donations that Mr. Trump had publicly boasted of turned out to have come from other people's pockets, like those who had given money to the Trump Foundation.

Three pages of Mr. Trump's income tax returns from 1995 obtained by The New York Times show that he claimed $916 million in losses.

Mr. Trump has repeatedly refused to release his federal income tax returns, defying the practice of presidential candidates going back four decades. He and his campaign have offered varying reasons, but the excuse most frequently invoked is that he is under audit by the Internal Revenue Service. The I.R.S. said that an audit does not prevent Mr. Trump from making his returns public.

Mr. Buffett made the same point. "I have been audited by the I.R.S. multiple times and am currently being audited," he wrote in the letter. "I have no problem in releasing my tax information while under audit. Neither would Mr. Trump — at least he would have no legal problem."

The Trump campaign had no comment on Mr. Buffett's letter.

Mr. Buffett's tax strategies were drawn into the debate when Mr. Trump blamed Mrs. Clinton for not doing more when she was a senator to fix the tax code and close loopholes that favored Wall Street and wealthy campaign donors. Mrs. Clinton, who has pledged to raise taxes on rich Americans, while Mr. Trump's plans would sharply reduce them, responded that a Republican-controlled Congress had repeatedly blocked such efforts.

Mr. Buffett declined to comment further on his letter. George Soros, another billionaire entrepreneur who has supported the Clinton campaign, was also singled out by Mr. Trump for claiming outsize deductions of $1.5 billion on his taxes. A spokesman for Mr. Soros, Michael Vachon, said he had no comment.

Mr. Buffett has frequently criticized tax laws and loopholes for enabling him to pay a smaller share of his income in taxes than his secretary. The so-called Buffett rule, which has been endorsed by Mrs. Clinton, would require people who earn more than $5 million to pay at least 30 percent of their income in taxes.

Mr. Buffett did concede that his tax payments have, at times, been much smaller. In 1944, he admitted, when he was just 13, "I owed only $7 in tax that year."

Forget Taxes, Warren Buffett Says. The Real Problem Is Health Care.

BY ANDREW ROSS SORKIN | MAY 8, 2017

OMAHA — "The tax system is not crippling our business around the world."

That was Warren E. Buffett, the chairman and chief executive of Berkshire Hathaway, over the weekend at the company's annual meeting, known as "Woodstock for capitalists."

Mr. Buffett, in a remarkably blunt and pointed remark, implicitly rebuked his fellow chief executives, who have been lobbying the Trump administration and Washington lawmakers to lower corporate taxes.

In truth, Mr. Buffett said, a specter much more sinister than corporate taxes is looming over American businesses: health care costs. And chief executives who have been maniacally focused on seeking relief from their tax bills would be smart to shift their attention to these costs, which are swelling and swallowing their profits.

It was clarifying to hear Mr. Buffett frame things this way. The need for corporate tax relief has become the lodestar of the corner office, with C.E.O.s rhapsodizing over President Trump's plan to try to stimulate growth by cutting tax rates for businesses.

But as Mr. Buffett pointed out, these chief executives are missing the bigger issue — the one that should be their Holy Grail. As a percentage of our gross domestic product, the cost of maintaining our American health care system — hospitals, H.M.O.s, doctor visits, prescription drugs, medical devices, insurance companies, Medicare — is rising at an alarming rate. And Corporate America pays a big (and growing) chunk of the bill.

We're not talking about the cost of health insurance, which is a fraction of the overall cost.

Today's corporate tax rates, Mr. Buffett seemed to suggest, are a distraction, not a true impediment to growth.

"If you go back to 1960 or thereabouts, corporate taxes were about 4 percent of G.D.P.," Mr. Buffett said. "I mean, they bounced around some. And now, they're about 2 percent of G.D.P."

By contrast, he said, while tax rates have fallen as a share of gross domestic product, health care costs have ballooned. About 50 years ago, he said, "health care was 5 percent of G.D.P., and now it's about 17 percent."

His is one of the most cogent arguments for renewing attention on the underlying costs of our health care system — an issue far beyond the debate around the Affordable Care Act and what it is going to look like if it is repealed and replaced.

Mr. Buffett said our global competitiveness had fallen largely because our businesses were paying far more for health care — a tax by another name — than those in other countries.

At his annual shareholders' conference, which drew tens of thousands of people to Omaha, he gave a virtual seminar on the economics of health care that chief executives and lawmakers would be helped by hearing. He demonstrated in stark terms that the constant refrain from the business community about taxes should probably be redirected toward trying to bend the cost curve of health care.

"When American business talks about strangling our competitiveness, or that sort of thing, they're talking about something that as a percentage of G.D.P. has gone down," Mr. Buffett said. "While medical costs, which are borne to a great extent by business," have swelled.

He is right: In 1960, corporate taxes in the United States were about 4 percent of G.D.P., which is probably the best way to measure the burden on businesses. Then the percentage fell steadily, reaching its bottom in 1983 before rising slightly over the last several decades. Today, it is 1.9 percent.

In the meantime, health care costs as a percent of G.D.P. have skyrocketed, significantly diverging with those of other industrial countries. Our health care costs stand at 17.1 percent of G.D.P., up from 13.1 percent in 1995.

The figure in Germany is only 11.3 percent, up from 9.4 percent during the same period. Japan's is 10.2 percent, up from 6.6 percent. Britain's health care costs are 9.1 percent of G.D.P., up from 6.7 percent in 1995. And China's is only at 5.5 percent, up from 3.5 percent.

That puts the United States at a material disadvantage far beyond the tax differential. And it harms American companies in particular, since they bear such a big share of those costs. Corporations spend $12,591 on average for coverage of a family of four, up 54 percent since 2005, according to a study by the Kaiser Family Foundation.

"Medical costs are the tapeworm of American economic competitiveness," Mr. Buffett said, using a metaphor he has employed in the past to describe the insidious and parasitic costs of our health care system.

Mr. Buffett is a Democrat, but his business partner, Charles T. Munger, is a Republican — and a rare one who has advocated a single-payer health care system. Under his plan, which Mr. Buffett agrees with, the United States would enact a sort of universal type of coverage for all citizens — perhaps along the lines of the Medicaid system — with an opt-out provision that would allow the wealthy to still get concierge medicine.

Our bloated health care system, Mr. Buffett asserted, is the true barrier to America's world competitiveness as well as "the single biggest variable where we keep getting more and more out of whack with the rest of the world."

But people don't talk about it enough. "It's very tough for political parties to attack it, but it's basically a political subject," Mr. Buffett said in reply to a question I had posed. (I was one of three journalists and three analysts who, along with shareholders, peppered Mr. Buffett and Mr. Munger with questions during the meeting.)

That's not to say corporate tax reform won't help, but it is tiny relative to fixing health care.

Indeed, Mr. Buffett said, even if Washington put in place a tax credit for capital investment, he did not think that BNSF — the railroad company he owns, which spends billions on fixing rail tracks — would do its job faster or better because of the potential tax credit.

"I can't recall sending anything out to our managers saying, 'Let's do this because the tax law is going to change,' " Mr. Buffett said.

Mr. Munger, the vice chairman of Berkshire Hathaway, added: "We're not going to change anything at the railroad just for some little tax jiggle."

Neither man, however, is expecting the bigger tax — health care — to be fixed anytime soon.

"On this issue, both parties hate each other so much that neither one can think rationally, and I don't think that helps, either," Mr. Munger said.

There's Only One Warren Buffett

BY ELISA MALA | MAY 7, 2018

The Berkshire Hathaway C.E.O.'s three-day extravaganza — er, shareholders' conference — drew tens of thousands of fans to Omaha.

OMAHA — Officially, it's known as the Berkshire Hathaway Annual Shareholders Meeting.

Unofficially, a handful of nicknames describe the three-day extravaganza that happens in the first weekend of May, in which tens of thousands of people descend upon Omaha to revel in all things Warren Buffett.

There's "Berkyville," which captures the folksy, small-town tenor of the event. There's "AGM," an abbreviation of "Annual General Meeting," preferred by the finance crowd. And there's Mr. Buffett's personal favorite: "Woodstock for capitalists."

But the most revealing name is the shortest one: the meeting. Just as some New Yorkers refer to the Big Apple as "the city," as if there were only one, scores of attendees consider this shareholders meeting to be in a class of its own.

In part, that's because the atmosphere feels closer to a carnival than a buttoned-up investors' conference. There are tables of merchandise and costumed mascots, Ping-Pong matches and a movie reel of celebrity-filled skits and spoofs. There is an unofficial circuit of V.I.P. parties and piggyback events. At the center of it all is Mr. Buffett, Berkshire Hathaway's chief executive, one of the world's most successful investors and the weekend's enthusiastic master of ceremonies.

"There's a cult of personality, and I mean that in a positive way," said Dan Calkins, the president and chief operating officer of Benjamin Moore.

For Alexis Ohanian, the co-founder of Initialized Capital and a former executive chairman of Reddit, the fun began long before he touched down in Nebraska. "There's such a range of people, even just from the plane out of Newark to here," he said. Pointing to his business partner, Garry Tan, he added, "This guy talked to, uh, well, I don't want to name drop."

As if on cue, the investor Li Lu walked up to shake Mr. Ohanian's hand; inches away, John Collison, the chief executive of Stripe, typed away on his laptop. For Mr. Tan, the big names mattered less than the Midwestern sensibilities: "There is a piece of this that really resonates with us, around being plain-spoken and investing in what you understand," he said.

The epicenter of the festivities is Omaha's CenturyLink Center exhibition space: One wing is fully devoted to booths of Berkshire Hathaway-owned brands. Friday is known as "shopping day." It's a dedicated opportunity for Mr. Buffett's admirers to buy his brands, snack on his preferred foods (See's Candies and Dilly Bars) and take selfies next to his various likenesses (or, in Mr. Tan's case, in an Oscar Mayer hot dog costume). Another wing is home to a Madison Square Garden-like arena, where the actual shareholders meeting is held on Saturday.

Revelers line up overnight to get in — or, in capitalist fashion, hire other people to stand in line for them. This year, many people expressed gratitude for the gentle breezes and sunshine, a welcome reprieve from the torrential rainstorms of past years. A handful of revelers were dressed up in bow ties and silver-glitter heels. Others climbed up poles to snap photos of the crowd.

By 7 a.m., attendees were streaming into the arena. Many purchased fluffy pretzels and pink beverages adorned with umbrellas from the concessions stands and settled in to be entertained. A parody of Jay-Z and Alicia Keys's "Empire State of Mind" blasted over the loudspeaker, but the lyrics were changed to: "In Berkshire, financial strength is where dreams are made of, there's nothing you can't do."

Then the "movie" started rolling.

As in previous years, Berkshire Hathaway had created a video reel of skits with celebrities, who ostensibly agree to participate for free. This year Katy Perry was one of about half a dozen big names on the screen, joking about the Left Shark debacle at the Super Bowl in 2015 and comparing the uncoordinated backup dancer to the Oracle of Omaha himself. The right shark, she said, was the one who showed up on time to rehearsal and got none of the credit — and that was Mr. Buffett's vice chairman Charlie Munger. The crowd applauded loudly.

After the Berkshire Hathaway board was announced and earnings were delivered, the most beloved portion of the show began: Mr. Buffett and Mr. Munger held a question-and-answer session, taking on topics like global politics and cryptocurrencies. Mr. Buffett dispensed wise advice and spoke with occasional self-effacing charm. Mr. Munger delivered deadpan one-liners that drew raucous laughs, including his comparison of virtual currencies to "turds."

"If you're interested in business, this is the bucket-list event," said James Weber, the chief executive of Brooks Sports. "It's just priceless."

For hard chargers in the financial industry, who are often laser-focused on performance, it's a reminder that business can be fun. "Every year that I come personally, I walk away energized," said Mr. Calkins of Benjamin Moore, who said he has attended the meeting 17 times.

Even after the main event was over, there was still plenty of weekend left to enjoy.

There was a picnic at Nebraska Furniture Mart, a 5K run and a chance to challenge Mr. Buffett in a game of Ping-Pong (he promised to "take all comers"). There were additional finance meetings, private dinner parties and an exclusive brunch held by Mr. Buffett at the country club.

"People aren't coming here because they're investing money," said Conner Van Fossen, an Air Force member who attended the event with his father, Jim Van Fossen, for the first time. "It's about the spectacle."

George Soros: When Hate Surges

OPINION | BY GEORGE SOROS | MARCH 16, 2017

PRESIDENT TRUMP HAS wasted no time in cracking down on immigration. He pledged to build a wall, hire 15,000 new Immigration and Customs Enforcement and Border Patrol agents and speedily deport millions of undocumented immigrants. He justified these actions by claiming that immigrants regularly flout the "rule of law and pose a threat." In his first speech to Congress, he directed the Department of Homeland Security to create a new office — Victims of Immigration Crime Engagement, or Voice — dedicated to helping victims of crimes perpetrated by "removable aliens."

I am an immigrant and an American citizen, and, as a philanthropist, have supported migrants all over the world for more than 30 years. Based on my experience and the facts, the president's approach to immigrants is just wrong — and a new round of court injunctions against Mr. Trump's latest proposed travel ban on people from six Muslim-majority countries suggests many in the federal judiciary agree. It does nothing to make America safer, while whipping up emotions against immigrants that have translated into an alarming surge in hate incidents all across our nation. My heart goes out to the victims of violence, whatever the source. But in the name of protecting the population from a relatively minor source of concern, he is branding all immigrants as criminals.

Contrary to Mr. Trump's claims, immigrants commit significantly less crime than native-born citizens. This has been borne out in study after study, using a wide range of methodologies, dating back decades. According to the nonpartisan American Immigration Council, the percentage of the population that is foreign-born grew to 13.1 percent from 7.9 percent between 1990 and 2013. F.B.I. data shows that the violent crime rate dropped 48 percent during that time and today remains near historic lows. A recent study by the Journal on Ethnicity in

Criminal Justice shows that immigrants actually drive down crime rates in the neighborhoods where they live.

But targeting immigrants and minorities with false and prejudicial rhetoric, as Mr. Trump has done during the campaign and in the early weeks of his presidency, has spurred a surge in hate acts against them. The Southern Poverty Law Center found that hate incidents reported in the first few weeks following Mr. Trump's victory were at levels normally seen over a six-month period. No community appears safe from this rash of hate — with reports like school bullying against Muslim children, stories of Latinos being harassed on the street and told to "go back to your country," attacks on blacks and gays, and the desecration of Jewish cemeteries. This is a country that prides itself on neighbors looking out for one another. In Donald Trump's America, we are increasingly at one another's throats.

As hate incidents surged after the election last fall, I announced a $10 million investment to provide legal and social services to victims of hate crimes, to encourage local organizations across the country to do the same and to propose improvements and new ideas. This week we opened our Hate Incident Database to monitor the scope and depth of hate incidents across the country.

Having survived the Nazi persecution of Jews in Hungary, I escaped from Soviet occupation at age 17 and made my way first to Britain and then to America. This is not the America that attracted me. I have seen the damage done when societies succumb to the fear of the "other." And I will do all I can to help preserve the openness, inclusiveness and diversity that represent our greatest strength.

Demonizing immigrants weakens our country. Fighting against hate crimes makes us grow stronger together.

GEORGE SOROS, an investor and philanthropist, is the chairman of the Open Society Foundations.

George Soros Transfers Billions to Open Society Foundations

BY DAVID GELLES | OCT. 17, 2017

GEORGE SOROS, the billionaire hedge fund manager and a major Democratic donor, has given $18 billion to his Open Society Foundations, one of the largest transfers of wealth ever made by a private donor to a single foundation.

The gift, made quietly over the past several years but disclosed only on Tuesday, has transformed Open Society into the second-biggest philanthropic organization in the United States, behind the Bill and Melinda Gates Foundation. It will also place Mr. Soros, a lightning rod for conservative critics, squarely in the middle of the social and political debates convulsing the country.

Founded by Mr. Soros more than 30 years ago, Open Society promotes democracy and human rights in more than 120 countries. In recent years, the organization has increased its attention on the United States, investing in programs to protect gays and lesbians and reduce abuses by the police.

The organization funded treatment centers during the 2014 Ebola outbreak, a center for Roma art and culture, and efforts to protect people in the United States from what it described as "a national wave of hate incidents" after the 2016 election. After that spike in hate crimes, Mr. Soros, 87, committed $10 million to preventing such violence.

"We must do something to push back against what's happening here," Mr. Soros said in November, lamenting what he called the "dark forces that have been awakened" by the election.

His political focus — including large donations to Hillary Clinton and other Democratic politicians — has made Mr. Soros a target of criticism from both the Republican establishment and fringe elements of the far right. The conservative website Breitbart, for example, has

George Soros at the offices of the Open Society Foundations in New York in 2014.

accused Mr. Soros of attempting to make Ireland a "pro-abortion country" and undermining the control of European countries over their borders.

"Given America's place in the world right now, I think he's making an enormous statement," said Eileen Heisman, chief executive of the National Philanthropic Trust, a nonprofit that works with foundations. "He has a very clear point of view and he's not trying to hide it."

Patrick Gaspard, the vice president of the Open Society Foundations, who will take over as president at the end of the year, said the election of President Trump had given the organization's work a new sense of urgency.

Mr. Gaspard specifically cited Mr. Trump's commission on voter fraud, a panel that has faced much criticism from Democrats and that Mr. Gaspard said "utterly lacks integrity." "Our work on equal access and protection is more vital than it's ever been," he said.

Mr. Soros's philanthropy is rooted in his past.

He lived in Nazi-occupied Hungary as a boy. With Budapest under Communist rule in 1947, he left for London and then the United States, where he found success on Wall Street.

In 1992, Mr. Soros made a $1 billion bet against the British pound, a trade that famously earned him the nickname "the man who broke the Bank of England" when his aggressive selling of the currency pushed the government to devalue the pound.

As his fortune grew, Mr. Soros began funding efforts to promote democracy and human rights, establishing the first Open Society foundation in Hungary in 1984. Mr. Soros took the name from a book by the philosopher Karl Popper, "Open Society and Its Enemies," in which he argued for democratic governance, free expression and respect for individual rights.

"He lived through Nazi Hungary," Ms. Heisman said. "He knows what it's like to live in a closed society."

Mr. Soros eventually became one of the biggest donors to Democrats, including Mrs. Clinton. During the last election cycle, Mr. Soros gave millions to super PACs that opposed Mr. Trump and supported other Democratic candidates and causes. He also bet big in the markets that Mr. Trump would lose the election, a wager that cost him about $1 billion.

For decades, Mr. Soros funded the Open Society Foundations through annual donations of around $800 million or $900 million per year. But beginning a few years ago, he increased his contributions as part of his estate planning, bringing the organization's endowment to about $18 billion this year. The total donation figure was first reported by The Wall Street Journal.

Mr. Soros is expected to contribute at least another $2 billion in the coming years.

"There is no foundation in the world, including the Ford Foundation, that has had more impact around the world than the Open Society Foundations in the last two decades," said Darren Walker, president of the Ford Foundation. "Because there is no part of the world that they have not been. Their footprint is deeper, wider and more impactful than any other social justice foundation in the world."

Despite the infusion by Mr. Soros, the foundation said it did not plan to increase the amount that it hands out in grants or via programs in the near future. Open Society already spends about $900 million annually on programs and grants, more than it is legally required to.

And Mr. Soros's fortune will still be managed by familiar hands. Soros Fund Management, the entity that manages the billionaire's personal fortune, is also responsible for overseeing the Open Society endowment's investments.

Mr. Soros remains closely involved in the foundation's work.

"I talk to George constantly, regularly," said Mr. Gaspard, the foundation's incoming president. "George is incredibly engaged on these issues."

This year, Mr. Soros has fended off attacks by the prime minister of Hungary, who has been displeased with a university that the Open Society Foundations funded there.

Mr. Gaspard said the public pressure did not bother the foundation's leadership.

"Since its inception, the Open Society Foundations has worked with leaders in civil society, whether they are the Roma in Eastern Europe or African-Americans in Cleveland, Ohio, who continue to be subject to a second-class form of justice," he said.

Stacy Palmer, editor of the Chronicle of Philanthropy, said that no matter how the billions were spent, the gift by Mr. Soros would keep him in the center of social and political debates for years to come.

"He has been so transparent about his views, so we know where he stands on these issues," she said. "This is going to fuel as much happiness as it is controversy."

How Vilification of George Soros Moved From the Fringes to the Mainstream

BY KENNETH P. VOGEL, SCOTT SHANE AND PATRICK KINGSLEY | OCT. 31, 2018

WASHINGTON — Hours after he was informed last week that an explosive device had been delivered to his suburban New York home, George Soros, the billionaire investor and Democratic donor, got on a call with colleagues to discuss yet another threat: the authoritarian Hungarian government's crackdown on a university he had founded.

The attempted attack in New York — subsequently determined to have been part of a wave of pipe bombs targeting prominent critics of President Trump — did not come up. But it was no coincidence that Mr. Soros would be facing intense opposition and threats at the same moment in two countries thousands of miles apart.

On both sides of the Atlantic, a loose network of activists and political figures on the right have spent years seeking to cast Mr. Soros not just as a well-heeled political opponent but also as the personification of all they detest. Employing barely coded anti-Semitism, they have built a warped portrayal of him as the mastermind of a "globalist" movement, a left-wing radical who would undermine the established order and a proponent of diluting the white, Christian nature of their societies through immigration.

In the process, they have pushed their version of Mr. Soros, 88, from the dark corners of the internet and talk radio to the very center of the political debate.

"Soros is vilified because he is effective," said Stephen K. Bannon, Mr. Trump's former campaign strategist and White House adviser, who is now trying to promote a coordinated nationalist movement across Europe and in the United States that explicitly aspires to mirror and counteract the influence Mr. Soros has built on the left.

"I only hope one day I'm as effective as he has been — and as vilified," Mr. Bannon said, calling threats like the pipe bomb "the admission ticket for playing in this arena."

On Fox News, in Republican fund-raising appeals and in research by conservative advocacy groups, his name is invoked as an all-purpose symbol of liberalism run amok.

Mr. Trump references him in Twitter posts and speeches as a donor to anti-Trump protesters, and the president's family and closest advisers sometimes go much further. Donald Trump Jr. retweeted a claim this year by the comedian Roseanne Barr that Mr. Soros is a Nazi. And the president's lawyer, Rudolph W. Giuliani, retweeted a comment saying that Mr. Soros is the Antichrist whose assets should be frozen.

In at least one case, the attacks made their way into United States government-funded media. The Spanish-language Radio Television Marti network, which broadcasts pro-United States content in Cuba, aired a report in May that is now the subject of a government investigation. The report called Mr. Soros a "multimillionaire Jew" of "flexible morals," who was "the architect of the financial collapse of 2008."

In the final days of the midterm election race, in which he is spending heavily to elect Democrats, Mr. Soros is being heatedly, if implausibly, cast as the financier of the immigrant caravan, a deep-state presence in the federal bureaucracy and the hidden hand behind the protests against Mr. Trump's Supreme Court nominee.

In Europe, the effort to demonize him has been both fueled and harnessed by nationalist leaders like Prime Minister Viktor Orban of Hungary and politicians in formerly communist countries like Macedonia, Albania and Russia.

"He's a banker, he's Jewish, he gives to Democrats — he's sort of a perfect storm for vilification by the right, here and in Europe," said Michael H. Posner, a human rights lawyer and former State Department official in the Obama administration.

Mr. Soros has given his main group, the Open Society Foundations, $32 billion for what it calls democracy-building efforts in the United

States and around the world. In addition, in the United States, Mr. Soros has personally contributed more than $75 million over the years to federal candidates and committees, according to Federal Election Commission and Internal Revenue Service records.

That qualifies him as one of the top disclosed donors to American political campaigns in the modern campaign finance era, and it does not include the many millions more he has donated to political non-profit groups that do not disclose their donors.

By contrast, the network of conservative donors led by the billion-aire industrialist brothers Charles G. and David H. Koch, who have been similarly attacked by some on the American left, has spent about $2 billion over the past decade on political and public policy advocacy.

A RISING PROFILE

Mr. Soros initially focused his activism on nurturing the democracies that emerged from the dissolution of the Soviet Union. But as he has evolved in the United States into a more traditional political operator, conservatives have become increasingly driven to discredit him — and, in turn, to use him to discredit the candidates and causes he supports — sometimes by exaggerating or mischaracterizing his role in actions taken by groups he helps to fund, and sometimes with imagery widely seen as anti-Semitic.

The closing advertisement for Mr. Trump's 2016 campaign featured Mr. Soros — as well as Janet L. Yellen, the chairwoman of the Federal Reserve at the time, and Lloyd Blankfein, the chief executive of Goldman Sachs, both of whom are Jewish — as examples of "global special interests" who enriched themselves on the backs of working Americans.

If anything, Mr. Soros has been elevated by Mr. Trump and his allies to even greater prominence in the narrative they have constructed for the closing weeks of the 2018 midterm elections. They have projected on to him key roles in both the threat they say is posed by the Central Americans making their way toward the United States border and what they characterized as Democratic "mobs" protesting the nomination of Brett M. Kavanaugh to the Supreme Court.

The National Republican Congressional Committee ran an ad in October in Minnesota suggesting that Mr. Soros, who is depicted sitting behind a pile of cash, "bankrolls" everything from "prima donna athletes protesting our anthem" to "left-wing mobs paid to riot in the streets." The ad links Mr. Soros to a local congressional candidate who worked at a think tank that has received funding from the Open Society Foundations.

Even after the authorities arrested a fervent Trump supporter and accused him of sending the pipe bombs to Mr. Soros and other critics, Republicans did not back away. The president grinned on Friday when supporters at the White House responded to his attacks on Democrats and "globalists" by chanting, "Lock 'em up," and yelling, "George Soros."

Mr. Soros's attackers in the United States and in Europe have increasingly found common cause in recent years.

The conservative legal organization Judicial Watch, which has received funding from major conservative donors, this year began an effort to expose United States government assistance for what the group considers Mr. Soros's "far-left agenda" in South America and Eastern Europe.

The group's research director, Chris Farrell, referred last week to the "Soros-occupied State Department" on Lou Dobbs's television program on Fox Business. Fox Business later condemned the remark and banned Mr. Farrell from further appearances. But criticisms of Mr. Soros have been amplified on both Fox Business and Fox News.

Judicial Watch's efforts pick up a theme pushed by Republican members of Congress in letters to the State Department and the United States Agency for International Development this year accusing Mr. Soros's Open Society Foundations of using taxpayer funding to push a liberal agenda in Albania, Colombia, Macedonia and Romania. A spokeswoman for the Soros group said the programs in question focus on issues that are consistent with "American ideals," like fighting corruption and promoting the rule of law.

The conservative party in Albania is represented in Washington by a lobbyist who is close to Senator Ted Cruz, Republican of Texas, who signed one such letter, while Mr. Orban's government has made payments to lobbyists and think tanks with connections to Mr. Trump's team.

ANTI-SEMITIC ATTACKS

Mr. Soros was born into a Jewish family in Hungary, and survived the Nazi occupation as a child in part by posing as the Christian godson of a government official.

After World War II, Mr. Soros fled Hungary for England as the Soviet Union consolidated control in his home country. He worked as a waiter and a railroad porter and studied at the London School of Economics, where he was deeply influenced by the theories of an Austrian philosopher who taught there, Karl Popper. Mr. Popper wrote about the consequences of what he called "closed" and "open" societies — concepts that shaped Mr. Soros's investment strategy and philanthropy for decades.

His daring investments in companies and currencies proved hugely lucrative, prompting The Economist to call him "surely the world's most intriguing investor" in 1987. His decision to short the British pound in 1992 earned his funds a reported profit of $1 billion.

By then, he was turning his attention to democracy-building in Eastern Europe.

Mr. Soros and his foundations supported groups and individuals seeking to bring down Communism, including the Solidarity and Charter 77 movements in Poland and Czechoslovakia. The leaders of both groups would later lead their countries in the post-Communist era.

In Hungary, Mr. Soros distributed photocopiers to universities and libraries as a means to fight government censorship, and he paid for dissidents to study in the West. The recipients included a young Mr. Orban, then a liberal activist.

Supporters of President Trump at a campaign rally in Nevada. The National Republican Congressional Committee is running an ad in Minnesota suggesting that Mr. Soros funds "left-wing mobs paid to riot in the streets."

After the end of the Cold War, with the Open Society Foundations as his main vehicle, Mr. Soros funded new work for destitute Soviet scientists in Russia, paid for free school breakfasts for Hungarian children and set up a college, the Central European University, that later drew the ire of Mr. Orban's government.

In the United States, where Mr. Soros was granted citizenship in the 1960s, Mr. Soros's efforts often won bipartisan applause. A professed admirer of President Ronald Reagan's efforts to topple Communist rule in Eastern Europe, Mr. Soros, who at the time described himself as a political independent, was seen by anti-Communist Republicans as a fellow freedom fighter.

As his activities grew more prominent in Europe, and he began funding drug reform efforts in the United States, he started being cast in the 1990s as a central figure in a shadowy Jewish cabal by extremist figures such as the fascist presidential candidate Lyndon H. LaRouche

Jr. and allies of repressive Eastern European leaders who were targeted by groups funded by Mr. Soros.

The theories were initially confined to the anti-Semitic fringe, though Mr. Soros is not closely associated with Jewish or Israeli causes, and in fact has been accused of being anti-Israel and was criticized by Prime Minister Benjamin Netanyahu.

Mr. Soros first became a major target for Republicans when he donated $27 million in the 2004 election cycle to an effort to defeat President George W. Bush, whose administration Mr. Soros condemned for rushing to war in Iraq and compared to Hitler's Nazi regime.

J. Dennis Hastert, Republican of Illinois, suggested in 2003, when he was House speaker, that the money that Mr. Soros was spending to defeat Mr. Bush "could be drug money." And in 2010, the talk show host Glenn Beck accused Mr. Soros of "helping send the Jews to the death camps," devoting three hourlong episodes of his top-rated Fox News show to a series branding Mr. Soros a "puppet master" intent on engineering a coup in the United States. The claims were repudiated by the Anti-Defamation League.

The efforts by Mr. Soros and a small band of wealthy donors to defeat Mr. Bush in 2004, while unsuccessful, later led to the creation of a network of major liberal donors that reshaped the American political left, marked Mr. Soros as a leading figure in Democratic politics and reinforced his status as a perennial election-time foil for the right.

"Back then, it was a handful of crackpots; it was considered fringe; and it was contained," said David Brock, the self-described right-wing hit man who switched sides and started a fleet of liberal groups to track conservative disinformation, including from hosts like Mr. Beck.

"But it started coming back with a vengeance during the 2016 campaign," said Mr. Brock, whose groups have received millions of dollars from Mr. Soros.

During the 2016 campaign, Mr. Soros had expressed even greater alarm about Mr. Trump than he had about Mr. Bush, and he donated more than $16 million to groups supporting Hillary Clinton.

Mr. Soros, his allies say, interprets the attacks from Mr. Trump, Mr. Orban and their supporters as an effort to intimidate him into backing down. But the intimidation has backfired, they say.

When friends reached out to express concern for his safety after the pipe bomb news broke, Mr. Soros, who was not there when the package was delivered, changed the subject to what he called "the damage" being done by the Trump administration, said his political adviser, Michael Vachon.

Mr. Vachon said that Mr. Soros in recent days has drawn a connection from the president's rhetorical attacks on his critics to the pipe bombs and even to the killing of 11 people on Saturday at a Pittsburgh synagogue.

In an email to The New York Times, Mr. Soros said he was grieving for the victims of the Pittsburgh shooting and their families. He added: "I came to this country to find refuge. I am deeply distressed that in America in 2018 Jews are being massacred just because they are Jewish."

A BIG 2018 ROLE

Mr. Soros has donated more than $15 million in this election cycle to support Democratic candidates at the federal level, according to election commission records, and he has also donated to nonprofits that do not disclose their donors.

Mr. Soros's representatives say he gave $1 million to one such group, the Democracy Integrity Project, which was established after the 2016 election to investigate foreign interference in elections and to research Mr. Trump's connections to Russian interests. Mr. Soros is considering additional donations to the group, which has paid for research from Fusion GPS, the firm behind the controversial dossier containing salacious claims about Mr. Trump's ties to Russia.

The very scale of his activities has given Republicans an opening to portray him as a nefarious driving force behind divisive political conflicts.

After two protesters confronted Senator Jeff Flake, Republican of Arizona, inside an elevator on Capitol Hill in late September and urged him to vote against Mr. Kavanaugh's nomination to the Supreme Court, Mr. Trump dismissed the protesters as Soros pawns.

"The very rude elevator screamers are paid professionals only looking to make Senators look bad," Mr. Trump wrote on Twitter. "Don't fall for it! Also, look at all of the professionally made identical signs. Paid for by Soros and others. These are not signs made in the basement from love! #Troublemakers."

One of the women did, in fact, work for a group called the Center for Popular Democracy, which has received significant funding from the Open Society Foundations. But the group said that neither it nor Mr. Soros had paid people to protest.

At the same time, his network of European nonprofit groups was increasingly making him a target of authoritarian leaders, including President Vladimir V. Putin of Russia and Mr. Orban in Hungary.

Mr. Soros's foundations have been banned from distributing funds in Russia, while Open Society chose to move its offices out of Hungary this year after a smear campaign by the Orban government. The Central European University announced last week that it may soon follow.

In a campaign this year, Mr. Orban's party ran an advertisement that depicted a smiling Mr. Soros, overlaid with the slogan: "Let's not let George Soros have the last laugh." Critics argued that the image was meant to remind viewers of the "Laughing Jew," a common anti-Semitic trope.

KENNETH P. VOGEL and SCOTT SHANE reported from Washington, and PATRICK KINGSLEY from Berlin.

George Soros Has Enemies. He's Fine With That.

BY ANDREW ROSS SORKIN | OCT. 25, 2019

In an interview, Mr. Soros explained why he thinks the tide is turning back to "globalists" like him and what might happen in the 2020 election.

GEORGE SOROS IS a billionaire philanthropist, a former currency trader, a liberal champion and — in certain circles — a boogeyman. That last label seems to be a badge of honor.

"I'm very proud of the enemies I have," he said in an interview in his apartment on New York's Upper East Side. "It's a perfect way to tell a dictator or a would-be dictator if he identifies me as an enemy."

The list of people who do seem to think of Mr. Soros as an enemy includes President Trump and his personal lawyer Rudolph Giuliani, the government of China, and an uncountable number of conspiracy theorists.

Their objections to Mr. Soros, 89, stem from his backing of liberal causes and super PACs that opposed Mr. Trump and supported Democratic candidates like Hillary Clinton, and his Open Society Foundation, which, funded by his billions, has supported democracy and human rights in some 120 countries, often opposing autocratic regimes.

There's also a substantial amount of anti-Semitism directed toward Mr. Soros, who was born into a Jewish family in Hungary.

Having just published a collection of essays this week, called "In Defense of Open Society," he acknowledged that his brand of "globalism" — which he takes to mean an integrated, global economy underpinned by the rule of law — is out of favor amid Mr. Trump's "America First" approach, the trade war, the debate over Brexit and escalating fighting in the Middle East.

Looking out a window with expansive views of Central Park, Mr. Soros spoke about China, Mr. Trump and who he thinks will face off against the president in next year's election.

Notably, Mr. Soros is convinced that the arc of history may soon turn back his way, that Mr. Trump's election and Brexit were the nadir of anti-globalism and that a backlash to that nationalism is coming.

"Trump is still doing a tremendous amount of damage," he said, lifting himself up a bit in his desk chair. "I mean, just the last week what he has done in the Middle East has been devastating for America's influence in the world," he said, referring to the withdrawal of American troops from Syria.

Mr. Trump "is an aberration, and he is clearly putting his personal interests ahead of the national interests," he said. "That's a fact."

His face brightening, he said: "I think it will contribute to his demise next year. So I am slightly predicting that things will turn around."

Mr. Soros's bet is that Senator Elizabeth Warren of Massachusetts will become the Democratic nominee to compete against Mr. Trump.

"She has emerged as the clear-cut person to beat," he said. "I don't take a public stance, but I do believe that she is the most qualified to be president."

He quickly added that he was not endorsing Ms. Warren, perhaps realizing that any comment construed as an endorsement is likely to be used by her opposition.

"I'm not endorsing anybody because I want to work with whoever," he said. "I don't express my views generally because I have to live with whoever the electorate chooses."

Yet when I pointed out that many billionaires and his peers on Wall Street consider Ms. Warren's policies — taxing the rich and tightly regulating banks — a threat to the capitalistic system in which he made his riches, he said he disagreed with his former colleagues and repeated his support of a tax on the wealthy. (Mr. Soros signed an open letter calling for an additional tax on the wealth of the richest Americans.)

"I am in favor of taxing the rich," he said, "including a wealth tax."

Pausing for a moment, he looked like he was searching for the right words to explain himself.

"A financier makes people suspicious," he said. "And it does create a moral problem for me. As I became so successful, it basically put a self-imposed constraint on me that actually interfered with making money."

Still, Mr. Soros batted away the idea that he and his Wall Street brethren had the political power and influence that was often ascribed to them — or at least that they would have less power in this election cycle than in previous ones.

"There are more Main Streets in America than there are Wall Streets. So I don't think that Wall Street, other than being a source of money, will have its way in choosing the president."

That may be his view, but money clearly matters in American politics, in part because a Supreme Court ruling on campaign finance allowed parties to raise huge sums, to spend on advertising and voter outreach. In the three months through September, Mr. Trump's re-election campaign and the Republican Party raised $125 million, a record.

Still, Mr. Soros said he saw signs that people were growing tired of nationalistic tendencies.

We discussed the outrage over the N.B.A.'s free-speech travails in China, and he said it demonstrated to the world just how dangerous closed societies could be.

"I consider Xi Jinping's China the worst threat to an open society," he said of China's president, repeating a declaration he made this year in Davos, Switzerland, that prompted China to retort, "We hope the relevant American can correct his attitude."

Mr. Soros, who has long encouraged free trade as a strategy to open up otherwise closed countries, said that the strategy had not worked in China the way he had expected and that more intervention was needed.

Mr. Soros, pointing a finger in the air, called China "a mortal enemy" and said the West gave it too much of the benefit of the doubt.

"We should recognize it: It's a different system. It's totally opposed to ours, diametrically opposed to ours," he said. Perhaps to qualify his words, he added: "I'm not anti-Chinese at all. I'm just anti Xi Jinping."

To him, the United States should pressure companies like Huawei to push China to open up. Otherwise, he suggested, not only will President Xi continue to close China off, but its development of new technologies like artificial intelligence will keep it that way for generations.

Alluding to the Rev. Dr. Martin Luther King Jr.'s famed quote, "The arc of the moral universe is long, but it bends toward justice," Mr. Soros took issue with idea that societies were predisposed toward being open.

"The arc of history doesn't follow its own course. It needs to be bent," he said. "I am really engaged in trying to bend it in the right direction."

ANDREW ROSS SORKIN is a columnist and the founder and editor-at-large of DealBook. He is a co-anchor of CNBC's Squawk Box and the author of "Too Big to Fail." He is also the co-creator of the Showtime drama series Billions.

CHAPTER 4

Conservative Billionaires: The Kochs, the Mercers and the DeVos Family

With the election of billionaire Donald Trump in 2016, new attention was paid to how wealthy donors influence the political landscape, from campaign contributions to lobbying, to the formation of super PACs. The articles in this chapter focus on the impact of three conservative families, the Koch brothers, the Mercers and the DeVos family, and how they use their fortunes to impact the landscape of American politics.

New Democratic Strategy Goes After Koch Brothers

BY ASHLEY PARKER | MARCH 5, 2014

WASHINGTON — Charles G. and David H. Koch, the billionaire brothers who are perhaps the best-known patrons of conservative Republican politics, are bespectacled and in their 70s. They look genial enough.

But Democrats are embarking on a broad effort that aims to unmask the press-shy siblings and portray them, instead, as a pair of villains bent on wrecking progressive politics.

On Thursday, the Democratic Senatorial Campaign Committee is starting a digital campaign that will use Internet ads and videos, as well as social media, to tie Republican Senate candidates to the policies and actions of the Koch brothers. Its slogan: "The G.O.P. is addicted to Koch" (pronounced coke).

Up first on the list is Alaska, where Democrats will try to link Dan Sullivan and Mead Treadwell, the Republican Senate candidates, to an oil refinery in the state owned by Koch Companies Public Sector. The refinery is set to cease gasoline and jet fuel production, which would lead to the layoffs of roughly 80 refinery workers.

Senator Harry Reid of Nevada, the majority leader, foreshadowed the campaign by taking to the Senate floor on Tuesday — an unusual move — for the second time in two weeks to accuse the Koch brothers of unfairly meddling in the political system by helping to pump more than $30 million so far in television advertising and other activities into the most competitive congressional races across the country. On Wednesday, he attacked them again during his weekly news conference.

Many of the ads by Americans for Prosperity, a conservative advocacy group backed by the Koch brothers, are especially critical of President Obama's signature health care law.

But whether the words of Mr. Reid, a member of an institution with historically low approval ratings, and even the efforts of other Democratic groups, will be any match for what the Kochs can spend remains an open and urgent question for Democrats.

"Harry Reid can stand on the floor at the United States Senate and howl at the moon all night long if he wants," said Ryan Williams, a Republican strategist. "But the reality is that he is powerless to stop millions of Americans from watching ads that tell the personal stories of real people who have been hurt by Obamacare. He's basically spitting in the ocean and fooling himself into thinking that he's making waves."

In an interview in his Senate office on Wednesday, Mr. Reid said his outspokenness against the Kochs stemmed from his concern for the middle class. "Right now, because of people like the two brothers, the rich are getting richer, the poor are getting poorer, and the middle class is getting squeezed out of existence," he said. "They're against everything that's good for America today."

Koch Industries, meanwhile, accused the Senate majority leader of trying to change the subject from what it says are the destructive Democratic policies that many of the ads it supports are simply highlighting.

"Attacking Koch is nothing new and appears to happen whenever Senator Reid and the Democratic leadership want to distract voters from their abysmal record and failure to meaningfully address the issues in this country," said Robert A. Tappan, director of external relations for Koch Industries. "Congress has a 13 percent approval rating for a reason. We are confident Americans will see through this tactic."

Mr. Reid said his focus on the Koch brothers was both personal and political.

"How could I do nothing? How could I let these people try to buy America?" he asked. "Don't I have an obligation, of someone that has been designated to run the Senate, to speak out when I see two people trying to buy America?"

Democrats say the strategy of spotlighting the Koch brothers' activities is politically shrewd. The majority leader was particularly struck by a presentation during a recent Senate Democratic retreat, which emphasized that one of the best ways to draw an effective contrast is to pick a villain, one of his aides said. And by scolding the Koch brothers, Mr. Reid is trying to draw them out, both to raise their public profile, and also to help rally the Democratic base.

The approach stems, in part, from Democratic-funded research showing that many voters believe the political system is rigged in favor of the superrich.

"Part of responding to these attacks that the Koch brothers are spending millions upon millions on is to make sure the voters understand who is behind them, and what's behind them," said Geoff Garin, a Democratic pollster. "And our research has shown pretty clearly that once voters recognize the source of the attacks, they tend to discount them substantially."

In 2012, Mr. Garin produced a research project for Patriot Majority PAC, an outside Democratic group, looking at the public awareness that swing voters and traditionally Democratic constituencies have of the Koch brothers. He found that his focus group respondents had an "overwhelmingly negative" reaction to the Kochs' political involvement, with their top concern being that "the Koch brothers' agenda will hurt average people and undermine the middle class."

Craig Varoga, who runs Patriot Majority, used Mr. Garin's findings to start a "Stop the Greed Agenda" campaign — which seeks to highlight what it views as "mega-billionaire special interests," such as the Kochs', around the country. He also plans to do more to spotlight the brothers' ideological agenda this year.

Senate Majority PAC, a group that supports Democratic Senate candidates, has also begun featuring the Koch brothers in their ads. An ad for Bruce Braley, a Democratic Senate candidate in Iowa, specifically warns of negative advertising by "out-of-state billionaires playing politics with health care." And an ad attacking Terri Lynn Land, a Republican Senate candidate in Michigan, even features black-and-white images of the Koch brothers. "Terri Lynn Land: Helping the powerful at our expense," says the ad's narrator at one point, as a photo of the brothers flashes in the background.

Mr. Reid, who is known for his halting, whispery speaking style, said he realized attacking the Koch brothers and their money might be a Sisyphean task, but he remains undaunted. "I'm going to — with my inadequate ability to speak and project — I'm going to do everything I can with my lack of talent to bring attention to those guys," he said.

Billion Dollar Babies

OPINION | BY GAIL COLLINS | MARCH 5, 2014

THE KOCH BROTHERS are in the news more than Justin Bieber.

This week, the billionaire siblings from Kansas made the top 10 in Forbes's list of wealthiest people on the planet. In fact, if you lump Charles and David Koch together, they're No. 1. Meanwhile, in the Senate, Majority Leader Harry Reid embarked on a rampage of anti-Koch speeches, denouncing the brothers as cancer-causing polluters who pour unlimited money into conservative political campaigns in an "un-American" attempt to subvert democracy.

Then Charles Koch gave an interview to The Wichita Business Journal! I know, I know. But given the supreme lowness of the brothers' low profile, it was an electric moment.

"Somebody has got to work to save the country and preserve a system of opportunity," Koch said, explaining his late-life calling as the nation's premier right-wing megadonor.

My question for today is: Do you think it's fair to call these guys oligarchs? We have been thinking about oligarchs lately since our attention has been fixed on the former Soviet Union, which is Oligarch Central. In fact, the new Ukrainian government just responded to the tensions in its eastern region by dispatching two billionaires to serve as provincial governors.

"Oligarch" sounds more interesting than "superrich person with undue political influence." The Koch brothers have a genius for being publicly boring, while plowing vast sums of money into political action groups designed to make it difficult for anybody to make a good estimate of how much they've given to promote their goal of, um, saving the country.

Maybe it would help focus the public mind if we started referring to them as the Wichita oligarchs.

We do need to focus. The country has had very rich folks trying to influence national policy forever. But these days they seem to be getting very richer by the moment, and thanks to the Supreme Court, there's no longer any real lid on what they can spend.

Who would you want to count as an oligarch? I'd definitely vote for any billionaires who underwrite campaigns against environmental regulation while their company shows up as No. 14 on the list of Toxic 100 Air Polluters. We're looking at you, Kochs. (Thank you for the information, Political Economy Research Institute, University of Massachusetts.)

Michael Bloomberg? Bloomberg bought himself 12 years as New York City mayor; his final election cost him more than $100 million, or $174 per vote, which sounds pretty darn oligarchic. Although when it comes to promoting a political career, being mayor will get you a good seat at a large number of parades.

Warren Buffett? He's richer than any individual Koch. But, I'm sorry. I do not see an oligarch running around demanding that the government raise his taxes.

I would definitely have voted for the late Harry Simmons of Texas, who donated $31 million to political action committees in the last presidential election cycle. The collapse of campaign finance laws was a big time-saver for Simmons, whose estranged daughter once said that he gave her $1,000 for each blank political contribution card she signed. But Simmons died last year, as did Bob Perry, a billionaire Texas realtor who shared Simmons's enthusiasm for that Swift Boat campaign against John Kerry.

"The question we're asking is: who's going to fill the oligarch vacuum?" said Craig McDonald of Texans for Public Justice. "And what do you call the level right under oligarchs? We've got plenty of them."

What comes below oligarchs? I guess mini-garchs. And below them, microgarchs. If you have a chance, try to refer to Donald Trump as a microgarch. It will drive him crazy.

But back to the real money: How about Paul Singer? He's a hedge fund billionaire who's sort of famous as the conservative donor who supports gay rights. As oligarchs go, however, he has a troubled track record: Rudy Giuliani in 2008, Chris Christie in 2012, Chris Christie, um, now.

Tom Steyer? This is another hedge fund billionaire. He's also an environmental activist who's investing $100 million in a fund to reward politicians who support climate change legislation and punish those who don't. The Center for Public Integrity, which dubs Steyer's new fund a "single-issue vanity super PAC," is not a fan. But at least he's not crusading for healthier hedge funds.

Sheldon Adelson? You remember Sheldon Adelson. He's the billionaire casino owner who's currently funding a campaign to combat online gambling. Adelson claims he's propelled by a "moral standard," which apparently involves saving betters from losing money in any venue that does not involve going to a casino. But we will always remember him as the guy who invested more than $16 million in the presidential prospects of Newt Gingrich.

This is truly only the billionaire beginning. Feel free to offer nominees. But don't get carried away. We want to be selective here. Start calling everybody an oligarch and it won't be special anymore. It'll just be like calling them lobbyists.

GAIL COLLINS joined The New York Times in 1995 as a member of the editorial board and later as an Op-Ed columnist. In 2001 she was appointed editorial page editor — the first woman to hold that post at The Times.

In Wichita, Koch Influence Is Revered and Reviled

BY CARL HULSE | JUNE 17, 2014

WICHITA, KAN. — In national politics, playing in Charles Koch's arena can mean saturation advertising against vulnerable Democrats, calls for tax cuts, demands to roll back government regulation and bitter clashes over climate change.

Here in the windswept hometown of the Koch family and Koch Industries, playing in Charles Koch Arena means something else entirely.

"I would be hard-pressed to find two things that are more important to this community than Koch Industries and Shocker basketball," said Gregg Marshall, coach of the Wichita State University men's team, which packs the arena, a house that Mr. Koch restored with his donations. "They put a nice chunk of change into this building."

Welcome to Kochville, where the family name conjures up something decidedly different from the specter raised by Democrats of secretive political operations funded by tens of millions of dollars in anonymous campaign money. For many living here in Wichita along the Arkansas River, it stands instead for well-paying jobs, extensive philanthropy like the $6 million for the arena renovation, and Kansas pride in being the headquarters of Koch Industries, the nation's second-largest privately held company, which produces oil, fertilizer and common household items.

Outside of Kochville, the brothers Charles and David Koch, whose worth is estimated at more than $50 billion each, are ready villains. Senator Harry Reid, Democrat of Nevada, the majority leader, regularly skewers them on the Senate floor. Others have proposed a constitutional amendment aimed at diluting their influence. The two are even the subject of an updated documentary titled "Koch Brothers Exposed: 2014 Edition."

The Koch Aquatic Center at the North Branch YMCA in Wichita, Kan.

But the charged atmosphere surrounding the Kochs elsewhere dissipates markedly in the city where their father, Fred Koch, started his business in 1925, even though the positive sentiment toward the Kochs is hardly universally shared.

The Kochs' reach in the city — once known as Cowtown because of its history as a railhead for Texas cattle drives and later called America's Air Capital for its private aircraft manufacturing indus- try — extends far beyond the arena and company headquarters now expanding in the northeast corner of the city.

Not far away is the Koch Community Plaza and Koch Scouting Center. Then there is the Koch Orangutan and Chimpanzee Habitat at the robustly Koch-supported Sedgwick County Zoo. Stop off for swimming lessons at the Koch Aquatic Center at the North Branch Y.M.C.A., or a learning experience recognizing the ecological interests of Fred Koch and his wife, Mary, at the Great Plains Nature Center's Koch Habitat Hall.

David Koch in 2011.

The Kochs contribute generously to Big Brothers Big Sisters, the Salvation Army and smaller community endeavors. The company's 3,500 jobs, regular employment opportunities and growth have meant steady paychecks in Wichita while other important and historic sectors of the local economy have struggled. The company estimated its direct payments in salary and benefits to Kansas workers, most of them in Wichita, at $410 million last year.

"There is almost no one in town who doesn't have a friend, a neighbor, a relative who works out at Koch," said Mary Beth Jarvis, a former Koch executive who oversees the organization that puts on the city's annual river festival and the accompanying symphony concert, which has long been underwritten by the Koch family.

Since 2000, organizations affiliated with the Koch family or company have given more than $50 million to Wichita and Kansas nonprofit groups, according to a company tally. Charles Koch lives in Wichita, and David lives in New York City, where he is also a donor to the arts and medicine.

While such strong community support has dazzled some residents, others see the Koch activities as insidious, an attempt to buy good will while the two brothers and their political allies spend much more behind the scenes to dismantle bedrock government programs more important to the average Kansan.

"That is all just bells and whistles, the shiny little things to distract you while they are proceeding to try to change our country into what they want it to be," said Randy Mousley, president of the Wichita teachers' union. He has clashed with Koch-backed groups and legislators over deep income and business tax cuts that reduced state aid for education and forced some districts to eliminate staff and raise property taxes.

"The Kochs are using their money and influence to hold our community hostage," said Louis Goseland, the campaign director for Kansas People's Action, a progressive activist group in Wichita that is also battling the Koch political agenda. "Right now we are working under Koch rule."

Koch officials dismiss such ideas as far-fetched. They say Koch contributions to Wichita are a way of repaying a city that has made it possible for both the Koch company and family to thrive because of its entrepreneurial spirit and available work force.

"We wouldn't do it just as protection money or whatever you call it," said Mark V. Holden, senior vice president and general counsel for Koch Industries. "It is not just about the business doing well. We are trying to get involved in issues and in places, particularly in this, our hometown, where we can make a difference."

Amplifying the company's influence, many former executives such as Ms. Jarvis, schooled in the Koch way, move on from the company to play leadership roles at other organizations in and around Wichita. Koch officials, present and former, sit on boards throughout the community.

"I don't think there has been a time since '95 that we have not had somebody from Koch Industries at an upper level on our board," said

Mark C. Reed, director of the zoo, who noted that it recently hosted the company's annual picnic for 4,000 employees and their families.

The philanthropic hand of the family was not always so visible as the Kochs used to shy away from recognition and kept their giving more low key. But escalating negative attention from a series of court fights and their rising conservative activism have spurred a more public role over the years, though Charles Koch only reluctantly let his name be affixed to the arena, officials said.

The company last week began a national advertising campaign around the theme "We Are Koch," emphasizing that Koch Industries was "started in the heartland" and had ample job opportunities.

The expansive local footprint of the company has left Koch critics to tread lightly. Mr. Mousley said he avoided the subject of the Kochs during family gatherings since his brother and sister-in-law work for Koch Industries. Some Wichita business owners and officials said they were reluctant to discuss the company's local reach for fear of losing business or good relations with neighbors.

Even Kansas People's Action chose to participate in a protest outside the Koch office in Washington rather than Wichita, where the company expansion and relocation of a major road (paid for entirely by the company) have pushed the public perimeter away from the office tower. Mr. Holden said the addition should enhance security around the headquarters after threats against the Kochs and their business. The company would not disclose the cost of the addition, intended to accommodate 745 employees, but the entire project is believed to have a price tag in excess of $100 million.

Mr. Holden said strong emotions had been stirred against the family since it escalated its political activities, citing the 2010 midterm elections as a turning point.

"I attribute a lot of that venom and invective and all that to the national political theater in which we're living now," said Mr. Holden, who added that Democrats, led by Mr. Reid, had seized on the Kochs as a convenient foil and fund-raising tool. "They don't have a bogyman like they do when there is a Republican presidential candidate, and so they have decided we are going to play that role."

As for those living in Wichita, the Koch dominance distresses some.

"My daughter, who just graduated from W.S.U., was telling me: 'Mom, what's here? The biggest thing you can aspire to do is work for the Koch brothers, and I don't want to do that,' " said Sulma Arias, the executive director of Kansas People's Action.

Others cannot reconcile the image of the Kochs as a sinister political force with their impression of Charles Koch as a regular guy who shows up at Shocker games with his family and meets once a year with Mr. Marshall, the coach, for a "state of the program" discussion.

"You see the name of our arena, so that sort of sums things up real quick," said Ron Baker, a Kansas native and star guard for the Shockers. "I've never met the guy, but I heard good things of him."

Jane Mayer's 'Dark Money,' About the Koch Brothers' Fortune and Influence

REVIEW | BY DAVID NASAW | JAN. 12, 2016

WHEN JANE MAYER published her 10,000-word article about Charles and David Koch in The New Yorker in August 2010, David Koch denounced her piece in print and, as she reports in her new book, "Dark Money: The Hidden History of the Billionaires Behind the Rise of the Radical Right," a "private investigative firm with powerful political and law enforcement connections was retained." While there was no hard evidence on who had hired the firm, "clues leading back to the Kochs were everywhere."

That effort may have backfired: Since that first article, Ms. Mayer has followed the trail of the tax-deductible "dark money" the brothers have secretly donated to political causes; absorbed the work of dozens of outstanding independent investigative journalists; ferreted out articles, speeches and interviews the brothers, or their advisers, have given, many of them quite revelatory; and secured access to previously unpublished sources.

"Dark Money," the result of Ms. Mayer's research, is a persuasive, timely and necessary story of the Koch brothers' empire. It may read overly long and include some familiar material, but only the most thoroughly documented, compendious account could do justice to the Kochs' bizarre and Byzantine family history and the scale and scope of their influence.

Ms. Mayer begins with Fred Koch, the family patriarch. "Oddly enough," she writes, "the fiercely libertarian Koch family owed part of its fortune to two of history's most infamous dictators, Joseph Stalin and Adolf Hitler," for whose regimes Mr. Koch's company built oil refineries in the 1930s.

Largely because of his experience in the Soviet Union, Fred Koch became a staunch anti-Communist and, in 1958, one of the 11 founding members of the John Birch Society. His son Charles did not fully commit himself to his father's political project until the mid-1970s, when, Ms. Mayer writes, Charles Koch "began planning a movement that could sweep the country." His declared goal? Nothing less than destroying what he referred to as "the prevalent statist paradigm."

The 1980 platform of the Libertarian Party, to which the Koch brothers provided financial support and on which David Koch ran for vice president, offered a preview of their anti-government zealotry. The Libertarians opposed federal income and capital gains taxes. They called for the repeal of campaign finance laws; they favored the abolition of Medicaid and Medicare and advocated the abolition of Social Security and the elimination of the Federal Election Commission, the Securities and Exchange Commission, the Environmental Protection Agency, the Food and Drug Administration and the Occupational Safety and Health Administration. "The platform was, in short," Ms. Mayer concludes, "an effort to repeal virtually every major political reform passed during the 20th century."

Not surprisingly, given the extremism of their views, which William F. Buckley Jr. characterized as "Anarcho-Totalitarianism," the Libertarians polled less than 1 percent of the votes. Ronald Reagan was elected president.

As Ms. Mayer notes, the Kochs, instead of accepting the voters' verdict, chose to spend money changing the way Americans voted. "During the next three decades," Ms. Mayer writes, "they contributed well over $100 million, much of it undisclosed, to dozens of seemingly independent organizations aimed at advancing their radical ideas."

When the Supreme Court in the 2010 Citizens United case permitted nonprofits to spend money on political campaigning, the Koch brothers funded their own political machine, which, in size, dollars and sophistication, rivaled that of the two major parties. Their success in the 2010 midterm election was remarkable, and, Ms. Mayer says, took the Democrats by surprise. Republicans picked up seats in the House and the Senate and 675 in state legislatures. "As a consequence of their

gains, Republicans now had four times as many districts to gerryman-
der as the Democrats" and the legislative power to pass a series of
laws suppressing the vote of those who might not support their agenda.

The Kochs, Ms. Mayer is careful to remind us, are only one of several fabulously wealthy families that have tried to move America to
the right. Their outsize influence is a result not only of their outsize
fortune — according to Forbes magazine, the brothers are the fifth and
sixth wealthiest Americans, with a combined family income larger
than that of Bill Gates — but also of their intellectual prowess and organizational skills. For more than a decade, they have organized donor
summits to which they have invited like-minded billionaires, political
consultants, media celebrities and elected officials. At these meetings,
plans are made, issues chosen, money raised, donations pooled, spending coordinated for the next election cycles.

The Koch brothers and their allies insist, and no doubt believe, that
their war on big government has been motivated by their commitment to the individual freedoms that government interferes with. Still,
"it was impossible not to notice," Ms. Mayer writes, "that the political policies they embraced benefited their own bottom lines first and
foremost. Lowering taxes and rolling back regulations, slashing the
welfare state and obliterating the limits on campaign spending might
or might not have helped others, but they most certainly strengthened
the hand of extreme donors with extreme wealth."

One of the more startling revelations in Ms. Mayer's book concerns
the number of billionaires in the Koch network who have had "serious past or ongoing legal problems" and whose companies have been
fined for violations of the Clean Air and the Clean Water Acts. Koch
Industries, she reports, has been perhaps the most flagrant and will-
ful polluter and scofflaw. According to the Environmental Protection
Agency's database, it was the No. 1 producer of toxic waste in the country in 2012.

To protect their investments in coal and oil pipelines and refineries
(somewhat pared down in the last decade), the Koch brothers have,

Ms. Mayer points out, funded think tanks committed to raising doubt about climate change. They have also spent tens of millions of dollars to roll back environmental regulations and defund or abolish the federal agencies that write and enforce them.

There are signs that the Kochs' influence may be waning. The Republican candidate they appeared to have favored, Gov. Scott Walker of Wisconsin, is no longer in the presidential race. Donald J. Trump, the candidate out in front, has made clear that he has no need for Koch money and has ridiculed those who "beg" for it. Still, as Ms. Mayer reports, twice as many Koch network dollars will be in play in 2016 than were in play in 2012: $889 million, only slightly less than the $1 billion that the Democratic and Republican national committees each expect to spend on the election.

Dark Money
The Hidden History of the Billionaires Behind the Rise of the Radical Right
By Jane Mayer
449 pages. Doubleday. $29.95.

DAVID NASAW is the Arthur M. Schlesinger Jr. Professor of History at the CUNY Graduate Center. His most recent book is "The Patriarch: The Remarkable Life and Turbulent Times of Joseph P. Kennedy."

How David Koch and His Brother Shaped American Politics

BY SHANE GOLDMACHER | AUG. 23, 2019

The billionaire, who died Friday, understood the power of changing "hearts and minds." He spent almost unlimited money on behalf of limited government.

IN 1980, DAVID H. KOCH, one of the two billionaire industrialist brothers at the center of a sprawling and powerful political network, served as the Libertarian Party's vice-presidential nominee. The ticket earned 1.1 percent.

But in the years since that failed run, Mr. Koch, who died on Friday, and his brother Charles, found far greater power and influence outside of elected office as they became two of the most prominent faces in a new era of megadonors in American politics, building a political apparatus that, at its peak, rivaled the Republican Party itself.

The Kochs and their network spent hundreds of millions of dollars in support of their particular brand of conservatism: One of limited government, more lenient immigration policy, free trade, free markets and limited corporate regulations — all while running Koch Industries, a conglomerate with annual revenues of $100 billion. But not long after they rose to become two of the most coveted political donors in America, they saw much of their worldview rejected by President Trump's ascendant version of the Republican Party.

Because so much of their network's money was funneled through an array of nonprofits, where full disclosure of finances is not required, it is near impossible to assess the full scope of their operations, but the influence is vast.

"The Koch brothers have been very strategically thinking about how best to shape politics over decades and at the same time they were amassing a fortune that would power whatever strategy they devised," said Sheila Krumholz, executive director of the Center for Responsive Politics, which tracks money in politics. She noted that they were especially effective working on narrow issues while pursuing a larger strategy.

"The Kochs," she said, "have built an empire."

THE FACE OF BIG MONEY

"If not us, who? If not now, when?" opened a letter from Charles G. Koch to donors in 2010, inviting them to join what the Kochs called their semiannual "seminars," gatherings of major contributors that would become the hallmark of the network.

The Koch-funded political operation would help propel the Tea Party takeover of Congress in 2010, spend an estimated $400 million on the 2012 campaign and fund heavily the Republican takeover of the Senate in 2014.

Along the way, the Kochs took full advantage after the Supreme Court sided with Citizens United and other rulings loosened spending rules. They became the most feared, recognized and loathed (by the left) Republican donors in the nation, surpassing even Karl Rove, as the boogeyman of Republican big money. In a sign of the vitriol around him, the hashtag #DavidKochisDeadParty was trending on Twitter Friday.

Matt Schlapp, who oversaw federal affairs for Koch Industries during President George W. Bush's second term and is now the chairman of the American Conservative Union, said the most lasting legacy of the Koch network will likely be its funding of a large network of think tanks and universities.

"I give the Kochs and their network high marks on understanding that if they don't change hearts and minds and build institutions that can educate people in the nonprofit world then the world will drift to the left, the government will continue to grow," Mr. Schlapp said.

He said their direct impact on politics was less pronounced. "The best judgment you can give it is mixed," he said. Part of that mixed legacy is linked to the rise of Mr. Trump. Some prominent alumni of Koch-funded organizations do hold high-ranking positions in the Trump administration. But the Kochs' approach to governance, beyond curbing business regulations and cutting taxes, has often been sidelined, if not rejected outright, by the Republican Party under President Trump, who dismissed the brothers as "a total joke" last year.

Trevor Potter, a former chairman of the Federal Election Commission and the current president of the Campaign Legal Center, a watchdog group, said the true Koch legacy was having "diminished our democracy."

"The Kochs changed two things. First, the system went from transparent spending to secret spending," Mr. Potter said. "The second was they were an important part of the wave of billionaires who took campaign spending to an entirely different level in American politics."

Both developments, he said, gave average Americans a deep sense of disenfranchisement.

'A HISTORICAL POWER PLAYER'

Parts of the Koch network have at one point touched on nearly every facet of the conservative movement. There have been separate organizations for outreach to Latinos (the LIBRE Initiative), veterans (Concerned Veterans for America), younger voters (Generation Opportunity) and older voters (60 Plus Association), for instance. A national political group, Americans for Prosperity, established outposts in the majority of states across the country.

"David Koch helped design and implement the center-right, free enterprise, activist wing of the political spectrum," said Scott Reed, the senior political strategist of the United States Chamber of Commerce. "And he became a historical power player."

The agenda for the 2010 Koch seminar was revealing. It included fighting "climate change alarmism and the move to socialized health care," as well as "the regulatory assault on energy" — issues that would recur over in the coming years.

In 2014, the Koch network was at the center of the successful Republican efforts to wrest control of the Senate from Democrats. A network of six Koch-linked nonprofits had paid to air nearly 44,000 television spots by August of that year, according to a study by the Center for Public Integrity.

Harry Reid, the Nevada Democrat who was then the Senate majority leader, took to the Senate floor in early 2014 to declare that "Senate Republicans are addicted to Koch" (the name is pronounced coke), as the network's television ads hammered Democrats in key races.

The sweeping Republican Senate victories that fall put Senator Mitch McConnell in power. He would use the majority to block some of President Obama's final judicial appointments, most notably forcing a vacancy on the Supreme Court for nearly a year until it was filled by President Trump's selection of Judge Neil Gorsuch in early 2017.

Environmental groups have denounced the Kochs, whose business empire includes oil operations, as "secretly funding the climate denial machine," as Greenpeace put it, adding up to $127 million in such spending over two decades. Among the recent Koch brothers pursuits has been killing mass transit projects around the country.

"If someone has the freedom to go where they want, do what they want," Tori Venable, Tennessee state director for Americans for Prosperity, told The New York Times last year, "they're not going to choose public transit."

The Kochs were perhaps at their peak in 2015, as the last Republican presidential primary was heating up. Koch officials outlined plans to spend as much as $900 million that cycle — possibly as much as the Republican Party itself. In a sign of their influence, Jeb Bush, Ted Cruz, Marco Rubio, Scott Walker and Carly Fiorina all trekked to a luxury hotel in Southern California to pitch the network's donors in person that summer.

"I, for one, cannot wait to see who the Koch brothers pick," President Obama joked at the White House Correspondents Association dinner that year.

'TWO NICE GUYS WITH BAD IDEAS'

But the Kochs did not get their pick. Instead, Mr. Trump would go on to win the nomination and redirect the party away from the Koch network's brand of fiscal conservatism, and their preference for free trade and a more open immigration policy. (The Kochs did spend millions supporting Mr. Trump's tax cut legislation.)

"Trump's passion was clearly focused on stopping immigration and stopping free trade and that was pretty well unacceptable to the Kochs," said David Boaz, executive vice president of the Cato Institute, a libertarian think tank that has long received money from the brothers.

In mid-2018, Charles Koch, without naming Mr. Trump, warned of the "rise of protectionism" and those who were "doing whatever they can to close themselves off from the new, hold on to the past, and prevent change."

Mr. Trump quickly responded. He attacked the brothers, saying they "have become a total joke in real Republican circles" with a "highly overrated" political network.

"Two nice guys with bad ideas," Mr. Trump wrote on Twitter.

In a shift last year, the Koch network ran ads in support of a Democratic senator, Heidi Heitkamp of North Dakota, who was being challenged by a staunch Trump supporter, Kevin Cramer. Mr. Cramer won the election. This year, the network has signaled plans to stay out of the White House contest entirely.

Yet even as the Kochs have receded somewhat from electoral politics, alumni of their network continue to hold sway in Mr. Trump's government. A former top Koch operative, Marc Short, for instance, served as Mr. Trump's legislative affairs director and is now chief of staff to Vice President Mike Pence. Mr. Schlapp's wife, Mercedes, is a senior White House official. And a former director of communications for Koch Industries, Matt Lloyd, is a senior adviser at the State Department.

"It is really hard to quantify their impact," Ms. Krumholz said of the Kochs. "It was enormous. It was pervasive."

SHANE GOLDMACHER is a national political reporter and was previously the chief political correspondent for the Metro Desk. Before joining The Times, he worked at Politico, where he covered national Republican politics and the 2016 presidential campaign.

How One Family's Deep Pockets Helped Reshape Donald Trump's Campaign

BY NICHOLAS CONFESSORE | AUG. 18, 2016

LAST WEEK, as Donald J. Trump endured one of the most tumultuous stretches of his presidential campaign, a few longtime allies in New York conservative circles met for dinner and a drink. As the evening progressed, the conversation turned to an inevitable topic: What would it take to give Mr. Trump his best shot at winning?

A few days later, one of the guests, Stephen K. Bannon, the executive chairman of Breitbart News, would become Mr. Trump's campaign chief in a sudden shake-up. But it was a guest without a formal role in the campaign, a conservative philanthropist named Rebekah Mercer, who has now become one of its most potent forces.

Mr. Bannon's ascension on Wednesday — urged on Mr. Trump by Ms. Mercer, among others — shows how a cadre of strategists, "super PACs" and political organizations quietly nurtured by her family have emerged to play a pivotal role in Mr. Trump's presidential campaign.

Over more than half a decade, Ms. Mercer's father, the New York investor Robert Mercer, has carved an idiosyncratic path through conservative politics, spending tens of millions of dollars to outflank his own party's consultant class and unnerve its established powers. His fortune has financed think tanks and insurgent candidates, super PACs and media watchdogs, lobbying groups and grass-roots organizations.

Many of them are now connected, one way or another, to Mr. Trump's presidential bid. Mr. Trump's new campaign manager, Kellyanne Conway, is a veteran Republican pollster who previously oversaw a super PAC financed by the Mercers. Mr. Bannon oversaw Breitbart, an outlet that has often amplified Mr. Trump's message and attacked

Donald Trump at a campaign event in West Bend, Wis., on Tuesday.

his perceived enemies. Mr. Mercer reportedly invested $10 million in Breitbart several years ago, and most likely still has a stake: A company sharing an address with Renaissance Technologies, the hedge fund Mr. Mercer helps lead, remains an investor in Breitbart, according to corporate documents filed in Delaware.

Mr. Trump is also relying on Cambridge Analytica, a voter data firm backed by Mr. Mercer, whose staff members are working with Mr. Trump's vendors to identify potential Trump supporters in the electorate, particularly among infrequent voters. A Mercer-backed super PAC supporting Mr. Trump is now being shepherded by David Bossie, a conservative activist whose own projects have been funded in part by the Mercers' family foundation, according to tax documents.

Mr. Bannon has worked particularly closely with the family in recent years.

"I think they have complete confidence, and rightly so, in Steve Bannon's decisions and what he brings to the table politically," Mr. Bossie said. "He has been smart and successful in running these different political operations. And those things have come to the Mercers' attention."

The Mercers, who rarely grant interviews, declined through a spokesman to comment. Mr. Mercer, 70, a mathematician and competitive poker player who spent his early career at I.B.M., joined Renaissance in the 1990s and rose to become the co-chief executive, earning hundreds of millions of dollars along the way. Today, he and his wife, Diana, live on a sprawling estate on Long Island's North Shore where, according to court records, he installed a $2.7 million model railroad set (and later sued the vendor for overcharging him).

Like many elite donors, the Mercers shun mainstream media attention — even while financing alternative outlets that provide content for conservative activists. That includes not just Breitbart, but also the self-described watchdog organization Media Research Center and the Government Accountability Institute, home to Peter Schweizer, the author of "Clinton Cash," a book examining the Clinton family philanthropies. (Mr. Bannon co-founded the institute and Ms. Mercer, 42, has served on its board; she also co-produced a documentary based on the book and released last month, just before the Democratic National Convention.)

They have given to libertarian organizations, such as the Cato Institute, and political organizations like the Club for Growth, which spends millions of dollars each election cycle in Republican primaries, hoping to promote orthodox conservative policies on taxes and spending. The Mercers are also significant donors to the sprawling political network overseen by the political activists Charles G. and David H. Koch, which is also libertarian-leaning.

But unlike the Koch brothers, who remained neutral in the Republican primary and have said their organizations will focus on congressional races this fall, the Mercers were deeply involved in the Republican nominating battle this year. And they have shown a taste for more bare-knuckled and populist politics than most of Mr. Mercer's fellow hedge fund magnates.

The family originally backed Senator Ted Cruz of Texas, a more traditional conservative but one who, like Mr. Trump, is disliked by much of the party establishment. During the early phase of the campaign, Mr. Mercer donated $13 million to a super PAC supporting Mr. Cruz. In doing so, he broke with many peers in the elite donor world, who looked to candidates like Jeb Bush or Senator Marco Rubio of Florida.

The Mercers maintained close control over the group's purse strings, installing Ms. Conway to oversee the group and coordinate with several other pro-Cruz groups, an unusual move for a super PAC. During the Republican primary, the group ran ads questioning Mr. Trump's conservative credentials, hoping to outflank Mr. Trump.

But the Mercers moved to support Mr. Trump after he won the nomination. They were helped in part, according to a person who asked for anonymity to describe the family's thinking, by Mr. Trump's growing emphasis on traditional conservative ideas, such as tax cuts. And the family broke with Mr. Cruz in highly public fashion after his speech at the Republican convention, when the Texas senator refused to endorse Mr. Trump and instead suggested that Republicans should "vote your conscience" for candidates "up and down the ticket."

In an extraordinary rebuke, the Mercers issued a rare public statement, calling themselves "profoundly disappointed" in Mr. Cruz.

In late June, the Mercer-financed super PAC quietly re-formed as Make America Number One, now a pro-Trump entity. Mr. Bossie, a longtime conservative activist who has produced documentaries about the Clinton family and illegal immigration, is leading the group, which is likely to raise more money from the Mercers to pay for attacks on Hillary Clinton.

MAGGIE HABERMAN and **JONATHAN MARTIN** contributed reporting.

Robert Mercer, Bannon Patron, Is Leaving Helm of $50 Billion Hedge Fund

BY MATTHEW GOLDSTEIN, KATE KELLY AND NICHOLAS CONFESSORE | NOV. 2, 2017

ROBERT MERCER, a billionaire investor and top financial backer of conservative causes, is stepping down as co-chief executive of Renaissance Technologies, as the giant hedge fund faces a backlash from some clients who resent Mr. Mercer's embrace of polarizing political figures.

Discomfort with Mr. Mercer's political activism — including protests aimed at university endowments, foundations and pension funds with money invested in Renaissance — has showed signs of taking a small but growing toll. The retirement fund for Baltimore's police and firefighters, for example, last week asked that all of the $33 million it had invested in Renaissance be refunded, said David A. Randall, the retirement fund's deputy executive director.

The Baltimore fund had been contacted by a local reporter about whether the pension was bothered by Mr. Mercer's political activities. Seeking to avoid bad publicity, the pension's directors convened an emergency conference call and decided to pull their money.

That $33 million withdrawal was a rounding error for Renaissance, which has more than $50 billion in assets. But it signaled a growing unease, inside and outside the firm, about Mr. Mercer's backing of Stephen K. Bannon, the former White House adviser. Renaissance's founder, James Simons, is a prominent Democratic booster who supported Hillary Clinton's presidential campaign.

In letters to investors and to Renaissance staff on Thursday morning, Mr. Mercer said he would step down as co-chief executive and as a board member on Jan. 1. He said he would remain involved with the research arm of Renaissance, which uses complex mathematical equations to create trading strategies.

Robert Mercer of the Renaissance Technologies hedge fund in Washington in March.

Mr. Mercer, 71, sought in his letter to employees to distance himself from Mr. Bannon, who has gone back to running Breitbart News, the divisive media outlet and hub for nationalist and far-right activism. He said he was selling his investment in Breitbart to his daughters, who also are active in conservative politics.

"I have great respect for Mr. Bannon, and from time to time I do discuss politics with him," Mr. Mercer wrote. "However, I make my own decisions with respect to whom I support politically. Those decisions do not always align with Mr. Bannon's."

His departure is not likely to fundamentally alter either Renaissance's status as one of the most profitable hedge funds or Mr. Mercer's status as one of the most sought-after financiers in the conservative eco-system. In fact, the firm took on $1 billion of new funds in the past month.

But it illustrates how the worlds of politics and business are colliding in the Donald Trump era. President Trump has tried to surround himself with corporate executives, but the president's actions and rhetoric have left some of these leaders facing angry customers and employees. A number of presidential advisory councils, for example, disbanded this summer as chief executives resigned in protest over Mr. Trump's lukewarm denunciations of white supremacists.

Mr. Mercer followed an unusual route to become arguably the most powerful person in the right-wing movement that thrust Mr. Trump into the White House.

A shy computer coder and model-train aficionado, he spent years at I.B.M. before joining Renaissance in 1993. He helped build the hedge fund into one of the industry's most successful firms.

Beyond donating to political campaigns, Mr. Mercer became a large financial backer of Cambridge Analytica, a voter-data firm that worked closely with the presidential campaign of Mr. Trump.

Lawmakers in Washington are scrutinizing Cambridge Analytica in connection with investigations into Russian meddling in the presidential election; the company has turned over documents to the House intelligence committee.

Mr. Mercer and his daughter Rebekah were instrumental in Breitbart's rise into a powerful force in conservative politics.

That backing has become controversial, partly because of the site's connections to white nationalists. One especially inflammatory Breitbart personality, Milo Yiannopoulos, reportedly has received financial support from the Mercers.

Mr. Mercer on Thursday distanced himself from Breitbart, Mr. Bannon and Mr. Yiannopoulos, who resigned from Breitbart earlier this year.

"Actions of and statements by Mr. Yiannopoulos have caused pain and divisiveness undermining the open and productive discourse that I had hoped to facilitate," Mr. Mercer wrote. "I was mistaken to have supported him, and for several weeks have been in the process of severing all ties with him."

Mr. Yiannopoulos said in a statement: "I am grateful for Bob's help in getting me this far in my career. I wish him and the family all the best."

Activist groups recently have pressured university investment funds to pull their money from Renaissance. The college Democratic organization at Michigan State University, for example, recently began calling on the university's endowment to withdraw its roughly $50 million investment.

This week, students at the State University of New York at Stony Brook on Long Island voiced concern about donations to the university from Mr. Mercer and Renaissance.

Mr. Randall of the Baltimore retirement fund compared the decision to redeem money from Renaissance to the decision of whether to invest in a tobacco company or gun manufacturer. He said Renaissance is one of the fund's best performing investments.

Not all investors were bothered by the controversy surrounding Mr. Mercer. The endowment for Michigan State has no plans to withdraw its money despite the campus protests, said Jason Cody, a university spokesman.

"We hire investment managers based on their long-term expected performance and fit for the overall portfolio," Mr. Cody said. "We do not consider the personal political opinions and private activities of individual employees when making decisions."

Steve Yoakum, executive director for Public School Retirement System of Missouri, another Renaissance investor, said the furor over Mr. Mercer was a "manufactured issue." He said performance trumped anything else.

Renaissance has made its investors lots of money. Its three main funds that are open to outside investors are up more than 10 percent through October this year. So far this year, the hedge fund has attracted about $10 billion in new assets.

The combination of Renaissance's consistently strong performances, its secretive nature and its leaders' idiosyncratic personalities have created an aura of mystique around the firm. Mr. Mercer's pivotal and prominent support for Mr. Trump shoved Renaissance into the spotlight.

For example Mr. Mercer hosts a well-known holiday costume party at his Long Island estate. Last year, the president-elect and a coterie of his top advisers were among the guests.

"Mercer is now such a controversial figure, that must cause all kinds of difficulties for the company," said Nick Patterson, a computational biologist at the Broad Institute, who hired Mr. Mercer at Renaissance. He said Mr. Mercer's prominence could make it harder for Renaissance to hire the best people.

Even as he steps down from Renaissance, Mr. Mercer is likely to accelerate his political giving in the future, according to people with knowledge of Mr. Mercer's thinking who were not authorized to speak publicly.

Without a day-to-day role in Renaissance management, these people said, Mr. Mercer would have more freedom and time to devote to his philanthropy and other activities, including an effort to recruit and support conservative candidates who want to replace the current Republican leadership in Congress.

Mr. Mercer's departure could stem investor defections from Renaissance. Mr. Randall said that with Mr. Mercer leaving, the Baltimore pension fund could reconsider its request to withdraw the $33 million.

"My professional position is I don't think this will be the last discussion concerning Renaissance," he said.

Additional reporting by **MICHAEL M. GRYNBAUM** in New York, **ALEXANDRA STEVENSON** in Hong Kong and **JEREMY W. PETERS** in Washington.

Betsy DeVos, Trump's Education Pick, Plays Hardball With Her Wealth

BY NOAM SCHEIBER | JAN. 9, 2017

AFTER TOM CASPERSON, a Republican state senator from Michigan's Upper Peninsula, began running for Congress in 2016, he assumed the family of Betsy DeVos, President-elect Donald J. Trump's nominee to be education secretary, would not oppose him.

The DeVoses, a dominant force in Michigan politics for decades with a fortune in the billions, had contributed to one of Mr. Casperson's earlier campaigns. But a week before his primary, family members sent $24,000 to one of his opponents, then poured $125,000 into a "super PAC," Concerned Taxpayers of America, that ran ads attacking him.

The reason, an intermediary told Mr. Casperson: his support from organized labor.

"Deceitful, dishonest and cowardly," was how Mr. Casperson's campaign described the ads, complaining that the groups running them "won't say who they are or where their money is coming from." On Primary Day, Mr. Casperson went down to defeat.

In announcing his intention to nominate Ms. DeVos, Mr. Trump described her as "a brilliant and passionate education advocate." Even critics characterized her as a dedicated, if misguided, activist for school reform. But that description understates both the breadth of Ms. DeVos's political interests and the influence she wields as part of her powerful family. More than anyone else who has joined the incoming Trump administration, she represents the combination of wealth, free-market ideology and political hardball associated with a better-known family of billionaires: Charles and David Koch.

"They have this moralized sense of the free market that leads to this total program to turn back the ideas of the New Deal, the welfare state," Kim Phillips-Fein, a historian who has written extensively about the conservative movement, said, describing the DeVoses.

Betsy DeVos with President-elect Donald Trump, who has selected her to be education secretary, at his golf club in Bedminster, N.J.

Ms. DeVos declined to be interviewed for this article.

Like the Kochs, the DeVoses are generous supporters of think tanks that evangelize for unrestrained capitalism, like Michigan's Acton Institute, and that rail against unions and back privatizing public services, like the Mackinac Center.

They have also funded national groups dedicated to cutting back the role of government, including the National Center for Policy Analysis (which has pushed for Social Security privatization and against environmental regulation) and the Institute for Justice (which challenges regulations in court and defends school vouchers). Both organizations have also received money from the Koch family.

Indeed, the DeVoses' education activism, which favors alternatives to traditional public schools, appears to derive from the same free-market views that inform their suspicion of government. And perhaps more than other right-wing billionaires, the DeVoses couple their seeding of ideological causes with an aggressive brand of political spending. Half a dozen or more extended family members frequently coordinate contributions to maximize their impact.

In the 2016 cycle alone, according to the Michigan Campaign Finance Network, the family spent roughly $14 million on political contributions to state and national candidates, parties, PACs and super PACs.

All of this would make Ms. DeVos — whose confirmation hearing has been delayed until next week amid mounting pressure that her government ethics review be completed beforehand — very different from past education secretaries.

"She is the most emblematic kind of oligarchic figure you can put in a cabinet position," said Jeffrey Winters, a political scientist at Northwestern University who studies economic elites. "What she and the Kochs have in common is the unbridled use of wealth power to achieve whatever political goals they have."

BIRTH OF A POWER COUPLE

Ms. DeVos, 59, grew up in Holland, Mich., the daughter of a conservative auto parts magnate who was an early funder of the Family Research Council, a conservative Christian group. When she married Dick DeVos in 1979, it was akin to a merger between two royal houses of western Michigan.

Her husband's father, Richard Sr., co-founder of the multilevel marketing company Amway, was an active member of the Christian Reformed Church that preached a mix of social conservatism and self-reliance. He once told the church's official magazine that Chicago's poor dwelled in slums because that was "the way they choose to live," according to a Washington Post story from the 1980s.

A fan of Rolls-Royces and pinkie rings, Richard Sr. wrote books with titles like "Ten Powerful Phrases for Positive People."

A similar air hung over his business. Amway sales representatives, which the company calls "independent business owners," make money both by selling the company's products — everything from perfume to toilet bowl cleaner — and by recruiting other sales representatives.

The Federal Trade Commission once investigated the company for running a pyramid scheme before concluding that it had misled potential recruits about how much they could expect to earn.

The flip side of the family's proselytizing for capitalism, according to Professor Phillips-Fein, has been an effort to dismantle much "that would counterbalance the power of economic elites."

Amway funded a nationwide ad campaign in the early 1980s, protesting high taxes and regulations. Not long after, the company pleaded guilty to cheating the Canadian government out of more than $20 million in revenue.

The family had a more winning public face in Dick DeVos, who combined the practiced empathy of a pitchman with the entitlement of an heir, spending over $30 million on an unsuccessful run for governor of Michigan in 2006. The Detroit Free Press described him that year as the wealthiest man to seek office in the state's modern history.

Betsy DeVos, who served as chairwoman of the Michigan Republican Party for most of the decade between 1996 and 2005, has often played the role of strategist in the relationship. She was a key adviser in her husband's run for governor and publicly brooded that he had been too gentlemanly in his first debate against the incumbent.

"He's very good with people, a retail politician who looks you in the eye, shakes your hand, listens to what you say," said Randy Richardville, a former Republican leader of the Michigan Senate, describing the couple's strengths. "I would never underestimate Betsy DeVos in a knife fight."

Ms. DeVos has sometimes lacked her husband's finesse, once famously blaming many of the state's economic woes on "high wages." She has won detractors, by their account, by browbeating legislators into voting her way.

"Betsy DeVos was like my 4-year-old granddaughter at the time," said Mike Pumford, a former Republican state representative who once clashed with her. "They were both sweet ladies as long as they kept hearing the word 'yes.' They turned into spoiled little brats when they were told 'no.' "

But Ms. DeVos has often made up for what she lacks in tact through sheer force of will.

Mr. Richardville said he and Ms. DeVos disagreed over term limits, which she supported as party chairwoman and he opposed: "I said, 'I don't think you should be setting policy. You should be supporting those of us who do make policy.' But she never backed down."

While Dick and Betsy DeVos appear to practice a more tolerant form of Christianity than their parents — Ms. DeVos has spoken out against anti-gay bigotry — as recently as the early 2000s they funded some groups like Focus on the Family, a large ministry that helps set the political agenda for conservative evangelicals. They have also backed groups that promote conservative values to students and Christian education, including one with ties to the Christian Reformed Church.

Their economic views are strikingly similar to the elder Mr. DeVos's.

According to federal disclosures, Amway, which Dick DeVos ran between 1993 and 2002, has lobbied frequently over the last 20 years to reduce or repeal the estate tax. Only the top 0.2 percent wealthiest estates paid the tax in 2015.

The company has also opposed crackdowns on tax shelters.

Ms. DeVos has been an outspoken defender of unlimited contributions known as soft money, which she described in a 1997 editorial as "hard-earned American dollars that Big Brother has yet to find a way to control."

After Congress later passed a major campaign finance reform bill, a nonprofit that Ms. DeVos helped to create and fund masterminded the strategy that produced Citizens United, the 2010 Supreme Court decision laying the groundwork for super PACs funded by corporations, unions and individuals to raise and spend unlimited amounts in elections.

And then there are the family's efforts to rein in the labor movement.

Through their contributions to think tanks like the Mackinac Center, as well as Mr. DeVos's direct prodding of Republican legislators, the family played a key role in helping pass Michigan's so-called right-to-work legislation in 2012. The legislation largely ended the requirement that workers pay fees to unions as a condition of employment.

Unions in the state bled members in 2014, the first full year the measure was in effect.

Allies say the DeVoses fight for their beliefs. "Betsy and Dick see themselves as principled conservatives," said Frederick Hess of the American Enterprise Institute. "It kind of seems healthy and admirable to give resources to folks who are going to fight for causes you believe in."

But the fights can appear to be as much about consolidating power as ideology. Unions were arguably the family's most formidable political opponent in Michigan, one of labor's traditional strongholds.

CHANGES IN MICHIGAN

The DeVos family's roots as education activists date back at least to when Richard DeVos Sr. was running Amway and an institute based at the company's headquarters trained teachers to inject free-market principles into their curriculum.

According to an interview Ms. DeVos gave to Philanthropy magazine, she and her husband became interested in education causes when they began visiting a Christian school that served low-income children in Grand Rapids in the 1980s.

"If we could choose the right school for our kids" — by which she appeared to mean primarily private schools — "it only seemed fair that they could do the same for theirs," she told the magazine.

The family spent millions of dollars on a ballot proposal in 2000 asking if Michigan should legalize vouchers, in which students can use taxpayer money to attend private schools.

Many critics, like the education historian Diane Ravitch, argue that the point of vouchers is to destroy public education and teachers' unions. The group Americans United for Separation of Church and State has documented how conservative Christians have long supported vouchers, which could fund religious schools.

After voters objected by more than a two-to-one ratio, Dick DeVos gave a speech at the Heritage Foundation saying such efforts would have to shift to state legislatures, where groups backed by deep-pocketed donors could offer "a political consequence for opposition, and political reward for support of education reform issues."

It is not unusual for the wealthy — who devote nearly 50 percent of their philanthropic dollars to education, according to the group Wealth-X — to spend aggressively in the political realm to impose their preferred reforms.

Even by these standards, however, the DeVoses stand out for the amount of money they spend trying to advance their goals through politics rather than philanthropy, such as research into reforms or subsidizing schools.

As Sarah Reckhow, an expert on education philanthropy at Michigan State University, put it: "The DeVoses are like: 'No, we know what we want. We don't need to have all this window dressing.' "

Ms. DeVos has led two nonprofits that have spent millions of dollars electing governors and legislators sympathetic to school vouchers around the country.

Matt Frendewey, a spokesman for one of the groups, said the efforts had frequently been bipartisan, and that the amount of money they had spent has been dwarfed by contributions from teachers' unions opposed to reform. Yet in Michigan, at least, the family's political strategy has not been subtle.

After he defied Ms. DeVos on a key charter school vote, Mr. Pumford, the former Republican legislator, survived an effort by the Great Lakes Education Project, a nonprofit the DeVoses bankrolled, to defeat him in his 2002 primary.

But shortly after, the House speaker told him the Education Committee chairmanship he coveted would not be forthcoming. "I said, 'Why?' " Mr. Pumford recalled. "He said: 'You know why. The DeVoses will walk away from us.' " Mr. Pumford added: "She told me that was going to happen."

(Rick Johnson, the House speaker, said he did not recall the conversation but also that he had not promised Mr. Pumford the chairmanship and would not have explained his reasons for withholding it.)

Over time, the Great Lakes Education Project helped elect Republican majorities sympathetic to the DeVoses' agenda. But the DeVoses' lobbyists and operatives also discovered less messy ways to advance legislation.

Late one night of their last workweek in 2015, the Michigan House and Senate were about to approve some uncontroversial changes to campaign finance law, when the bill abruptly grew by more than 40 pages.

After the legislators discovered what they had voted for, many said they were horrified.

Tucked away in the new pages was a provision that would have made it much harder for local bodies like school boards to raise money through property tax increases.

"Michigan schools will likely suffer the brunt of the impact because the vast majority rely on periodic voter approval of local operating levy renewals for property taxes," the ratings agency Moody's wrote of the measure the following month.

"I was fooled into voting for something I opposed," said Dave Pagel, a Republican representative. "I consider it the worst vote I've made."

The chief culprits, according to Mr. Pagel and others at the state Capitol when the bill passed, were lobbyists closely tied to the DeVoses.

Tony Daunt, a spokesman for the Michigan Freedom Fund, a nonprofit headed by the DeVoses' longtime political aide, and whose political spending arm they have funded generously, said the group was "part of the discussion process with people in the legislature" about the proposal and "had consistently expressed support for the policy."

The law was later blocked by a federal judge, but the group has vowed to try again.

RADICAL SUSPICIONS

Ms. DeVos's advocates see in these fights the toughness to take on entrenched opponents of expanding reforms like charter schools and vouchers.

In promoting Ms. DeVos in The Washington Post, Mitt Romney, the Republican Party's 2012 presidential nominee, emphasized that her wealth gave her the independence to be "someone who isn't financially biased shaping education." He added, "DeVos doesn't need the job now, nor will she be looking for an education job later."

But critics see someone with an unmistakable agenda. "The signs are there that she will do something radical," said Jack Jennings, a former general counsel for the House education committee. "Trump wouldn't have appointed this woman for this position if he didn't intend something radical."

NOAH WEILAND contributed reporting. **DORIS BURKE** contributed research.

No Profit in Betsy DeVos

OPINION | BY GAIL COLLINS | OCT. 27, 2017

PERHAPS YOU'RE WONDERING how Betsy DeVos is doing.

Or maybe not, unless you're planning to go to a Halloween party dressed as the secretary of education.

DeVos is the superrich Republican donor who once led a crusade to reform troubled Michigan public schools by turning them into truly terrible private ones. Now she's in the Trump cabinet, and she seems to be dedicating a lot of her time to, um, lowering higher education.

"When no one was watching she hired a lot of people that come from the for-profit colleges," complained Senator Patty Murray of Washington, who feels the additions are far more interested in protecting their old associates than in overseeing them. Murray is the top Democrat on the Health, Education, Labor and Pensions Committee, otherwise known as HELP. These days it's hard to tell whether that's a promise of assistance or a cry of distress.

To oversee the critical issue of fraud in higher education, DeVos picked Julian Schmoke Jr., whose former job was a dean of — yes! — a for-profit university. Specifically a school named DeVry. Last year, under fire from state prosecutors and the Federal Trade Commission, DeVry agreed to pay $100 million to students who complained that they had been misled by its recruitment pitch.

That sort of thing is getting to be common in the darkest corners of the for-profit world. For instance, there's a now-defunct "university" that promised to show students how to get rich quick in real estate and wound up paying $25 million to settle the case. ...

Back to the Department of Education. One of DeVos's top advisers, Robert Eitel, is on a leave of absence from a company that operates for-profits and once paid more than $30 million to settle charges of deceiving students about the loans they were getting.

Which is, again, even more than that real estate school, where some students claimed they were encouraged by instructors to increase the limits on their credit cards. …

There are well over 3,000 for-profit colleges and universities in the country, everything from tiny schools that promise to set you off on a career in cosmetology to conglomerates with campuses all over the world. Some of them have names that might seem intended to be confused with somebody else's. (Not necessarily thinking of you, Brown College, Berkeley College, Columbia Southern University or Northwestern College.)

Experts say some for-profits are fine. However, there have been a ton of horror shows in which low-income men and women are promised a path to life-changing jobs but wind up with nothing to show except huge loan bills.

ITT Technical Institute in Florida gave students the impression they'd be having careers along the line of "C.S.I.: Miami." Actually, they frequently wound up working as security guards, degree in hand and $50,000 in debt.

There are so many awful for-profit school stories. There was that one in New York that sold students a $35,000 "Gold Elite Package" and had to change its name to "Entrepreneur Initiative" after the state determined it had no right to call itself a university. …

"The outcomes for people who take out loans at for-profits are abysmal," said Ben Miller of the Center for American Progress. He added that almost all the students borrow, for courses they could sometimes get for one sixth the price at a community college. And about half the people who borrow default.

As the stories about deceitful for-profits mounted, the Obama administration came up with regulations making it easier for students to refuse to pay their loans if a school had misrepresented their chances of graduating and getting a lucrative career. The rules were supposed to go into effect in July, but DeVos has delayed their implementation.

Insiders call those regulations "borrower defense to repayment." However, if you prefer, you could also refer to them as "something that reminds us of a certain school that used to promise its students fabulous careers in the real estate industry. ..."

O.K., we're talking here about Trump University. I knew I couldn't fool you forever. Cynics might wonder if DeVos has been going to the defense of for-profit colleges so quickly because she wants to please her boss. Who might not enjoy seeing a lot of headlines about greedy colleges that make promises they never intended to keep, being brought down by the forces of justice.

But let's be positive. Perhaps we could be grateful that DeVos is giving us opportunities to bring up Trump University on a regular basis. As a sort of cautionary tale.

For instance, the Department of Education has stopped approving new fraud claims against for-profits, leaving a backlog of more than 87,000. Every time the number goes up, we could say, "This is even more than the number of students who complained about their loans for Trump University."

If DeVos says what the country needs now is less regulation, we can recall that Trump University had instructors allegedly handpicked by Donald Trump himself, although it turned out that he'd never even met them.

Consider it a teaching moment.

GAIL COLLINS joined The New York Times in 1995 as a member of the editorial board and later as an Op-Ed columnist. In 2001 she was appointed editorial page editor — the first woman to hold that post at The Times.

The DeVos School for the Promotion of Student Debt

EDITORIAL | BY THE NEW YORK TIMES | AUG. 26, 2018

The education secretary is working hard to protect the scandal-ridden for-profit education industry from accountability.

SAY THIS FOR Betsy DeVos: The secretary of education has shown an impressive commitment to rescuing her friends in the for-profit college business from pesky measures to rein in their predatory behavior. As pet projects go, it lacks the sulfurous originality of her emerging idea to let states use federal dollars to put guns in schools. But it is a scandal nonetheless. Given the choice between protecting low-income students — and, by extension, American taxpayers — and facilitating the buck-raking of a scandal-ridden industry, Ms. DeVos aggressively pursues Option B.

This summer has been a fertile period for the secretary. A couple of weeks back, her department formally introduced its plan to jettison so-called gainful employment rules. These 2014 regulations require that, to receive federal student-aid dollars, for-profit colleges — along with certain programs at nonprofit and public institutions — must maintain a reasonable debt-to-income ratio among graduates. If a program's attendees typically rack up massive student debts and then cannot find decent jobs, the program is deemed a failure. Programs that fail in two out of three years become ineligible to receive the taxpayer-backed loans and grants with which so many students finance their schooling. The rules also require for-profit programs to make clear in their promotional materials whether or not they meet federal job-placement standards.

Ms. DeVos, delighting industry executives, promptly hit the pause button on these regulations upon assuming her post. Now the pending demise of the rules has been made official. Ms. DeVos contends that the system, put in place by President Barack Obama after bloody battles with the for-profit college industry and congressional Republicans, capriciously targets the sector. She has had far less to say about the industry's eye-popping overrepresentation in fraud complaints. A recent review of "borrower defense claims" — requests for loan relief filed with the Education Department by students asserting they were defrauded or misled by their schools — found that almost 99 percent involved for-profit institutions.

In recent years, for-profit colleges have been swamped by lawsuits charging that they use deceptive marketing practices and high-pressure recruitment tactics to snooker students into taking on crippling debt in the pursuit of worthless degrees. Two industry giants, ITT Technical Institute and Corinthian Colleges, have collapsed under the weight of the legal claims and government inquiries.

Dozens of additional programs have shut their doors of late rather than attempt to meet the new accountability standards. Consumer advocates see this as evidence that the common-sense regulations are working. Industry executives, and Ms. DeVos, see it as proof that the Obama administration had it in for the sector.

Gainful employment rules are but a piece of the accountability puzzle that Ms. DeVos is looking to end. In late July, the department announced it was tightening rules governing the forgiveness of student loans, also put in place by the Obama administration, increasing the burden of proof on individuals to show that they've been misled intentionally by their schools or that they've suffered grave financial hardship. Ms. DeVos has made clear her views of the forgiveness plan hammered out by the Obama administration — and of students seeking debt relief: "Under the previous rules, all one had to do was raise his or her hands to be entitled to so-called free money," she said.

The secretary insists that she wants to root out bad actors as much as anyone. But if that were true, she probably wouldn't have dismantled the department's team tasked with investigating fraud at for-profit schools. She also might have opted not to end her department's information-sharing arrangement with the Consumer Financial Protection Bureau, which is among the agencies that regulates this industry. (Until the Trump era, it was one of the most aggressive to do so.)

This problem affects not just students taken in by the schools' false claims, but also taxpayers who foot the bill for defaulted student loans. By the Education Department's own figures, repealing the Obama-era rules will cost taxpayers $5.3 billion over the next decade.

Ms. DeVos is a fan of using government money to fund private schools while demanding little accountability. It is no coincidence that she packed her department with aides with ties to for-profit colleges. One ex-industry executive, Robert Eitel, is a senior adviser who was involved in suspending the loan-forgiveness rules that are now being rewritten. Another hire, Julian Schmoke, is a former dean for the DeVry Education Group. Under President Obama, DeVry was being investigated by the department's special fraud unit. The inquiry was abandoned shortly after President Trump took office in 2017, and, that summer, Ms. DeVos put Mr. Schmoke in charge of the unit. (Mr. Schmoke will, the department has assured the public, recuse himself from issues involving DeVry.)

Under Ms. DeVos, the department also has halted investigations into Bridgepoint Education and the Career Education Corporation. Former executives and counselors for those companies now hold senior positions at the department.

All of them, of course, work for Mr. Trump, whose namesake "university" eventually paid $25 million to settle fraud claims of its own.

This is what happens when an administration stocks its agencies with people whose allegiances are to the industries they are meant to oversee. Mr. Trump's Environmental Protection Agency, for instance, has begun to resemble less a regulatory body than a convention of fossil-fuel fan boys. Former administrator Scott Pruitt was an unabashed cheerleader for oil and gas. His replacement, Andrew Wheeler, is a former coal lobbyist. On Monday, he proposed a rollback of the Obama administration's Clean Power Plan, which aimed to curb the release of greenhouse gases from power plants.

Ms. DeVos's plan to ax the gainful employment rules was entered into the Federal Register on Aug. 14, officially starting the 30-day period open to public comment on the proposed changes.

Barring an unforeseen twist, executives in the for-profit education industry will soon be sleeping better, secure in the knowledge that even the worst are no longer at risk of being thrown off their taxpayer-backed gravy train, no matter how epically they fail their students.

The editorial board represents the opinions of the board, its editor and the publisher. It is separate from the newsroom and the Op-Ed section.

Glossary

antitrust law   Regulations by the state and federal governments designed to protect fair competition in the market.

behemoth   Something huge or monstrous; an enormous and powerful organization.

capitalism   An economic and political system in which private individuals own trade and industry for profit.

conglomerate   A corporation made up of a number of different, seemingly unrelated businesses.

globalization   The process by which businesses develop international operations and spread influence on a global scale.

hedge fund   An official partnership of investors who pool their funds in order to gain more return on their profit.

income inequality   An extreme disparity in the distribution of income between individuals, leaving a high concentration of income in the hands of a small percentage of the population.

libertarianism   A political philosophy that maximizes personal liberty and autonomy over any collective responsibility.

lobbying   The practice of attempting to influence the actions and decisions of political officials toward the interest of a particular group or company.

lodestar   A star used to guide the course of a ship; a person or thing that serves as an inspiration or guide.

loophole   An ambiguity or omission in a text or contract through which the intent or purpose of a responsibility can be evaded.

Marxism The political theories of Karl Marx and Friedrich Engels that seek to examine the damaging impacts of capitalism on labor.

mogul An important, rich or powerful person.

oligarchy A power structure in which a small group of people, especially of the wealthy class, control the interests of a country or an organization.

philanthropy The act of donating money to charitable causes.

populism A political stance that appeals to the general public who feel that their interests are being overlooked in favor of those of the elite or wealthy classes.

redistribution The distribution of assets in a different way, intended to alleviate disparities in wealth and to achieve greater social equality.

regulation A official rule that regulates a process, activity or organization.

shareholder An individual or organization that holds stock in and therefore owns a share of a public or private organization.

super PAC A political action committee that is allowed to raise and spend funds indirectly, thereby exploiting a loophole to exceed the legal limits for political campaign donations.

wealth tax A tax on the total value of personal assets rather than on an individual's annual income.

Media Literacy Terms

"Media literacy" refers to the ability to access, understand, critically assess and create media. The following terms are important components of media literacy, and they will help you critically engage with the articles in this title.

angle The aspect of a news story that a journalist focuses on and develops.

attribution The method by which a source is identified or by which facts and information are assigned to the person who provided them.

balance Principle of journalism that both perspectives of an argument should be presented in a fair way.

bias A disposition of prejudice in favor of a certain idea, person or perspective.

commentary A type of story that is an expression of opinion on recent events by a journalist generally known as a commentator.

credibility The quality of being trustworthy and believable, said of a journalistic source.

editorial Article of opinion or interpretation.

fake news A fictional or made-up story presented in the style of a legitimate news story, intended to deceive readers; also commonly used to criticize legitimate news that one dislikes because of its perspective or unfavorable coverage of a subject.

feature story Article designed to entertain as well as to inform.

headline Type, usually 18 point or larger, used to introduce a story.

impartiality Principle of journalism that a story should not reflect a journalist's bias and should contain balance.

intention The motive or reason behind something, such as the publication of a news story.

interview story A type of story in which the facts are gathered primarily by interviewing another person or persons.

motive The reason behind something, such as the publication of a news story or a source's perspective on an issue.

news story An article or style of expository writing that reports news, generally in a straightforward fashion and without editorial comment.

op-ed An opinion piece that reflects a prominent individual's opinion on a topic of interest.

paraphrase The summary of an individual's words, with attribution, rather than a direct quotation of their exact words.

plagiarism An attempt to pass another person's work as one's own without attribution.

quotation The use of an individual's exact words indicated by the use of quotation marks and proper attribution.

reliability The quality of being dependable and accurate, said of a journalistic source.

rhetorical device Technique in writing intending to persuade the reader or communicate a message from a certain perspective.

source The origin of the information reported in journalism.

tone A manner of expression in writing or speech.

Media Literacy Questions

1. Identify the various sources cited in the article "How David Koch and His Brother Shaped American Politics" (on page 181). How does Shane Goldmacher attribute information to each of these sources in his article? How effective are Goldmacher's attributions in helping the reader identify his sources?

2. In "Why Don't Rich People Just Stop Working?" (on page 57), Alex Williams directly quotes Mark Zuckerberg. What are the strengths of the use of a direct quote as opposed to a paraphrase? What are the weaknesses?

3. Compare the headlines of "Why Jeff Bezos Should Push for Nobody to Get as Rich as Jeff Bezos" (on page 85) and "Billion Dollar Babies" (on page 168). Which is a more compelling headline, and why? How could the less compelling headline be changed to better draw the reader's interest?

4. What type of story is "Jeff Bezos, Mr. Amazon, Steps Out" (on page 71)? Can you identify another article in this collection that is the same type of story? What elements helped you come to your conclusion?

5. Does Carl Hulse demonstrate the journalistic principle of balance in his article "In Wichita, Koch Influence Is Revered and Reviled" (on page 171)? If so, how did he do so? If not, what could Hulse have included to make his article more balanced?

6. The article "Abolish Billionaires" (on page 34) is an example of an op-ed. Identify how Farhad Manjoo's attitude and tone help convey his opinion on the topic.

7. Does "How Vilification of George Soros Moved From the Fringes to the Mainstream" (on page 151) use multiple sources? What are the strengths of using multiple sources in a journalistic piece? What are the weaknesses of relying heavily on only one or a few sources?

8. Analyze the authors' reporting in "New Democratic Strategy Goes After Koch Brothers" (on page 164) and "How One Family's Deep Pockets Helped Reshape Donald Trump's Campaign" (on page 186). Do you think one journalist is more impartial in their reporting than the other? If so, why do you think so?

9. Often, as a news story develops, a journalist's attitude toward the subject may change. Compare "Warren Buffett Holds Forth on Sharing the Wealth" (on page 132) and "Forget Taxes, Warren Buffett Says. The Real Problem Is Health Care." (on page 138), both by Andrew Ross Sorkin. Did new information discovered between the publication of these two articles change Sorkin's perspective?

10. Identify each of the sources in "A Message From the Billionaire's Club: Tax Us" (on page 50) as a primary source or a secondary source. Evaluate the reliability and credibility of each source. How does your evaluation of each source change your perspective on this article?

Citations

All citations in this list are formatted according to the Modern Language Association's (MLA) style guide.

BOOK CITATION

THE NEW YORK TIMES EDITORIAL STAFF. *American Billionaires: Privilege, Politics and Power.* New York Times Educational Publishing, 2021.

ONLINE ARTICLE CITATIONS

BOWLEY, GRANT. "Winfrey Gives $12 Million to New Smithsonian Museum of Black History and Culture." *The New York Times*, 12 June 2013, https://artsbeat.blogs.nytimes.com/2013/06/12/oprah-gives-12-million-to-new-smithsonian-museum-of-black-history-and-culture.

BUFFETT, WARREN E. "Buy American. I Am." *The New York Times*, 16 Oct. 2008, https://www.nytimes.com/2008/10/17/opinion/17buffett.html.

BURNS, ALEXANDER, AND AMY CHOZICK. "Oprah 2020? Democrats Swing From Giddy to Skeptical at the Prospect." *The New York Times*, 8 Jan. 2018, https://www.nytimes.com/2018/01/08/us/politics/oprah-president-2020.html.

CHOZICK, AMY. "How Jeff Bezos Went to Hollywood and Lost Control." *The New York Times*, 2 Mar. 2019, https://www.nytimes.com/2019/03/02/business/jeff-bezos-lauren-sanchez-amazon-hollywood.html.

COHEN, PATRICIA. "Buffett Calls Trump's Bluff and Releases His Tax Data." *The New York Times*, 10 Oct. 2016, https://www.nytimes.com/2016/10/11/business/buffett-calls-trumps-bluff-and-releases-his-tax-return.html.

COHEN, PATRICIA. "A Message From the Billionaire's Club: Tax Us." *The New York Times*, 24 June 2019, https://www.nytimes.com/2019/06/24/business/economy/wealth-tax-letter.html.

COLLINS, GAIL. "Billion Dollar Babies." *The New York Times*, 5 Mar. 2014, https://www.nytimes.com/2014/03/06/opinion/collins-billion-dollar-babies.html.

COLLINS, GAIL. "No Profit in Betsy DeVos." *The New York Times*, 27 Oct. 2017, https://www.nytimes.com/2017/10/27/opinion/betsy-devos-for-profit -colleges.html.

CONFESSORE, NICHOLAS. "How One Family's Deep Pockets Helped Reshape Donald Trump's Campaign." *The New York Times*, 18 Aug. 2016, https:// www.nytimes.com/2016/08/19/us/politics/robert-mercer-donald-trump -donor.html.

CONLIN, JENNIFER. "The Tao of Oprah." *The New York Times*, 10 Oct. 2014, https://www.nytimes.com/2014/10/12/fashion/oprah-winfrey-hits-the -road-with-her-life-you-want-weekend-tour.html.

CORKERY, MICHAEL. "Where the Billionaires Come From." *The New York Times*, 19 Feb. 2017, https://www.nytimes.com/2017/02/19/your-money /where-the-billionaires-come-from.html.

DOWD, MAUREEN. "America's Billionaire." *The New York Times*, 21 Sept. 2013, https://www.nytimes.com/2013/09/22/opinion/sunday/dowd-americas -billionaire.html.

FEUER, ALAN. "Billionaires to the Barricades." *The New York Times*, 3 July 2015, https://www.nytimes.com/2015/07/05/opinion/sunday /billionaires-to-the-barricades.html.

GELLES, DAVID. "George Soros Transfers Billions to Open Society Founda- tions." *The New York Times*, 17 Oct. 2017, https://www.nytimes.com /2017/10/17/business/george-soros-open-society-foundations.html.

GELLES, DAVID. "Giving Away Billions as Fast as They Can." *The New York Times*, 20 Oct. 2017, https://www.nytimes.com/2017/10/20/business /soros-charity-zuckerberg-gates.html.

GOLDMACHER, SHANE. "How David Koch and His Brother Shaped American Politics." *The New York Times*, 23 Aug. 2019, https://www.nytimes.com /2019/08/23/us/politics/david-koch-republican-politics.html.

GOLDSTEIN, MATTHEW, ET AL. "Robert Mercer, Bannon Patron, Is Leaving Helm of $50 Billion Hedge Fund." *The New York Times*, 2 Nov. 2017, https:// www.nytimes.com/2017/11/02/business/robert-mercer-renaissance.html.

HAUGHNEY, CHRISTINE. "Oprah at a Crossroads." *The New York Times*, 25 Nov. 2012, https://www.nytimes.com/2012/11/26/business/media /oprah-winfrey-seeks-to-bolster-a-flagging-empire.html.

HULSE, CARL. "In Wichita, Koch Influence Is Revered and Reviled." *The New York Times*, 17 June 2014, https://www.nytimes.com/2014/06/18 /us/koch-brothers-donate-heavily-in-kansas.html.

KRUGMAN, PAUL. "Privilege, Pathology and Power." *The New York Times*, 1 Jan. 2016, https://www.nytimes.com/2016/01/01/opinion/privilege-pathology-and-power.html.

LEONHARDT, DAVID. "The Rich Really Do Pay Lower Taxes Than You." *The New York Times*, 6 Oct. 2019, https://www.nytimes.com/interactive/2019/10/06/opinion/income-tax-rate-wealthy.html.

MALA, ELISA. "There's Only One Warren Buffett." *The New York Times*, 7 May 2018, https://www.nytimes.com/2018/05/07/style/warren-buffett-omaha.html.

MANJOO, FARHAD. "Abolish Billionaires." *The New York Times*, 6 Feb. 2019, https://www.nytimes.com/2019/02/06/opinion/abolish-billionaires-tax.html.

MANJOO, FARHAD. "Why Jeff Bezos Should Push for Nobody to Get as Rich as Jeff Bezos." *The New York Times*, 19 Sept. 2018, https://www.nytimes.com/2018/09/19/technology/bezos-amazon-rich-concentration.html.

MULLANY, GERRY. "World's 8 Richest Have as Much Wealth as Bottom Half, Oxfam Says." *The New York Times*, 16 Jan. 2017, https://www.nytimes.com/2017/01/16/world/eight-richest-wealth-oxfam.html.

NASAW, DAVID. "Jane Mayer's 'Dark Money,' About the Koch Brothers' Fortune and Influence." *The New York Times*, 12 Jan. 2016, https://www.nytimes.com/2016/01/13/books/review-jane-mayers-dark-money-about-the-koch-brothers-fortune-and-influence.html.

THE NEW YORK TIMES. "The DeVos School for the Promotion of Student Debt." *The New York Times*, 26 Aug. 2018, https://www.nytimes.com/2018/08/26/opinion/editorials/betsy-devos-student-debt.html.

NOCERA, JOE. "How Warren Buffett Does It." *The New York Times*, 3 Mar. 2015, https://www.nytimes.com/2015/03/03/opinion/joe-nocera-how-warren-buffett-does-it.html.

O'BRIEN, TIMOTHY L., AND STEPHANIE SAUL. "Buffett to Give Bulk of His Fortune to Gates Charity." *The New York Times*, 26 June 2006, https://www.nytimes.com/2006/06/26/business/26buffett.html.

PARKER, ASHLEY. "New Democratic Strategy Goes After Koch Brothers." *The New York Times*, 5 Mar. 2014, https://www.nytimes.com/2014/03/06/us/politics/new-democratic-strategy-goes-after-koch-brothers.html.

SCHEIBER, NOAM. "Betsy DeVos, Trump's Education Pick, Plays Hardball With Her Wealth." *The New York Times*, 9 Jan. 2017, https://www.nytimes.com/2017/01/09/us/politics/betsy-devos-education-secretary.html.

SORKIN, ANDREW ROSS. "Forget Taxes, Warren Buffett Says. The Real Problem Is Health Care." *The New York Times*, 8 May 2017, https://www.nytimes.com/2017/05/08/business/dealbook/09dealbook-sorkin-warren-buffett.html.

SORKIN, ANDREW ROSS. "George Soros Has Enemies. He's Fine With That." *The New York Times*, 25 Oct. 2019, https://www.nytimes.com/2019/10/25/business/dealbook/george-soros-interview.html.

SORKIN, ANDREW ROSS. "Warren Buffett Holds Forth on Sharing the Wealth." *The New York Times*, 2 May 2016, https://www.nytimes.com/2016/05/03/business/dealbook/at-berkshire-hathaway-meeting-warren-buffett-talks-of-sharing-the-wealth.html.

SOROS, GEORGE. "George Soros: When Hate Surges." *The New York Times*, 16 Mar. 2017, https://www.nytimes.com/2017/03/16/opinion/george-soros-when-hate-surges.html.

STREITFELD, DAVID. "Amazon Hits $1,000,000,000,000 in Value, Following Apple." *The New York Times*, 4 Sept. 2018, https://www.nytimes.com/2018/09/04/technology/amazon-stock-price-1-trillion-value.html.

SULZBERGER, A. G. "A Quiet Meeting of America's Very Richest." *The New York Times*, 20 May 2009, https://www.nytimes.com/2009/05/21/nyregion/21summit.html.

TURKEWITZ, JULIE. "Who Gets to Own the West?" *The New York Times*, 22 June 2019, https://www.nytimes.com/2019/06/22/us/wilks-brothers-fracking-business.html.

VOGEL, KENNETH P., ET AL. "How Vilification of George Soros Moved From the Fringes to the Mainstream." *The New York Times*, 31 Oct. 2018, https://www.nytimes.com/2018/10/31/us/politics/george-soros-bombs-trump.html.

WEISE, KAREN. "Jeff Bezos, Amazon C.E.O., and MacKenzie Bezos Finalize Divorce Details." *The New York Times*, 4 Apr. 2019, https://www.nytimes.com/2019/04/04/technology/bezos-divorce-mackenzie.html.

WILKINSON, WILL. "Don't Abolish Billionaires." *The New York Times*, 21 Feb. 2019, https://www.nytimes.com/2019/02/21/opinion/billionaires-innovation.html.

WILLIAMS, ALEX. "Why Don't Rich People Just Stop Working?" *The New York Times*, 17 Oct. 2019, https://www.nytimes.com/2019/10/17/style/rich-people-things.html.

WINGFIELD, NICK. "Jeff Bezos Wants Ideas for Philanthropy, So He Asked Twitter." *The New York Times*, 15 June 2017, https://www.nytimes.com/2017/06/15/technology/jeff-bezos-amazon-twitter-charity.html.

WINGFIELD, NICK. "Move Over, Bill Gates. Jeff Bezos Gets a Turn as World's Richest Person." *The New York Times*, 27 June 2017, https://www.nytimes.com/2017/07/27/business/jeff-bezos-richest-man.html.

WINGFIELD, NICK, AND NELLIE BOWLES. "Jeff Bezos, Mr. Amazon, Steps Out." *The New York Times*, 12 Jan. 2018, https://www.nytimes.com/2018/01/12/technology/jeff-bezos-amazon.html.

Index